Opening Doors within the Margin

Opening
Doors within
the Margin

Sean O'Brien

authorHOUSE®

AuthorHouse™
1663 Liberty Drive
Bloomington, IN 47403
www.authorhouse.com
Phone: 1-800-839-8640

Published by AuthorHouse   05/20/2013

ISBN: 978-1-4817-5572-6 (sc)
ISBN: 978-1-4817-5571-9 (hc)
ISBN: 978-1-4817-5570-2 (e)

Library of Congress Control Number: 2013909411

Contents

Acknowledgments

It is my pleasure to honorably mention the actual experts and professionals that I have been able to work along side throughout this process. I want to dedicate this effort to them. They are: Jay Kinder, Michael Reese, John Kitchens, Stace Bohlender, Reedy Daly, Tracy Combs, Carla Romo, Ashley Geiger, Caitlin Jones, Hollie Hewes, Sue Cabelka, Katrina Raether, Adrianne Arrington, Annette Gallion, Darlene Anderson, Megan Cabral, Kari Hiner, Epiphany Silverio, Tina Fritts, and Russ Boen. This is the team that for the most part, makes up or supports the laboratory often referred to as "Jay Kinder Real Estate Experts". These people are the absolute best at what they do, and they have the numbers to prove it.

It goes without saying that the thoughts or methods demonstrated within this work are solely the thoughts of the author and are not necessarily shared or practiced by the members of Jay Kinder Real Estate Experts or NAEA.

Introduction

To say that selling your home will cause a lot of anxiety is in incredible understatement. Do you hang your strategy on the basis of an appraisal that was done a few years ago? Do you do an Internet search and try to associate some practical meaning to the letters "CMA"? Do you have any understanding of the actual market conditions; not only surrounding your general community, but your actual neighborhood? What are the socio-economic factors that are "just common knowledge" to a real estate professional?

The simple answer is that none of these factors will *actually* be researched or developed by your agent; but those factors will however, be discussed to the point that your head starts to spin . . . then, based on a whirlwind demonstration, you give the expert or professional (depending on what franchise you are dealing with at the time) a small amount of rapport. Regardless of whether you are a buyer or a seller, you have just gone through the first qualifying "cut". Your interest and motivation has been identified for later use.

If you are a seller within this "negotiation" you will have already most likely negotiated away as much as 7.5% of your home's selling price. Interestingly, you haven't yet even been prepared for the discussion of abstracting fees or treatment/replacement/repairs (TRRs) that will be identified during the home inspection. You will be asked to correct these issues depending on appraisal requirements. You will probably also be asked to cover all of the buyer closing costs as well as purchase some sort of a home warranty for the major appliances on the buyer's behalf.

That said the passage of a home or property sale is a relatively simple process. What I would like to do is simply pull the curtain back and expose the industry, in a non-threatening manner, to demonstrate what actually takes place outside of the things that a buyer or a seller generally see. These are the margins that real estate "professionals" dwell within, and depending on your level of personal commitment; you may be someone that will benefit in saving a large portion of that prior mentioned 7+% by taking advantage of the same systems.

I am leading into the reality that if you are selling your home, a real estate professional or expert will negotiate with you in some manner to determine the compensation that you will provide to both the listing and the selling brokerage involved in the potential sale of your home.

I have personally negotiated as much as a 7.5% compensation agreement that the seller is responsible to pay regardless of the actual sales price. Based on my ability to convince that seller that I know what the heck I am talking about, they will likely agree to a compensation factor of 7.5%. If the home sells for $225,000, the compensation to my brokerage is a value of $16,875, which equals 4% of the sales price for the listing and 3.5% to the sale.

"My" negotiation with you puts your selling net earnings at $208,125. This is before any inspection or lender required repairs, or any closing costs or home warranties. Now, add $2500 for repairs (just a top end cap estimate) and another $8000 or so for buyer closing costs. Your net has now diminished to $197,625. That is a 12.2% reduction from your sales price to your net. Remember that percentage, you will see it again.

What this means is that if your principle mortgage pay-off is $197,625, you will need to sell it for at least $220,000. That $22,375 difference could be considered sales-side equity, as it is equity that you are writing off; yet will not be writing off until it has been realized within a $220,000 sales price. $22,375 represents a worse case scenario in which you the seller will come up with every buyer side concession possible.

To put a point on this, that $22,375 also represents 7 years of house payments, likely at a rate of 5% over 30 years (or more simply, you made nearly 80 payments). It is scary to think that it is really possible to negotiate years of mortgage payments away from you in a matter of minutes.

On a brighter note, there are some factors that you can actually plan on as I mentioned. If you are a buyer and are using a mortgage lender, you can't get away from inspection or appraisal requirements. As a seller, you should also want to help the buyer with their closing if need be (abstracting/title insurance/gap checks, etc.), but not necessarily their prepaid expenses (hazard insurance and tax escrows); but where does this leave you?

In the model above, you can meet the minimum buyer/seller requirements by only investing roughly 5%, or $11,250 as opposed to $22,375 that you would have. The difference is $11,125 that is yours if YOU would like to earn it.

How? Like I said, I'd like to pull back the curtain "so to speak", and allow you to see all of the inner workings of what real estate "professionals" do on a daily basis. Frighteningly so, I think that despite the figures that I just demonstrated to you, you will agree that these professionals are worth every penny if the situation calls for it; but if you are up to it, that $11,125 margin might be something that you would be interested in saving for yourself.

Ok fine, but who do I sell my home to?

Chapter 1

Lead Generation

So, Mr. Buyer, you want to buy a house? You get on-line, cruise though any number of websites, all of which provide you with enough of a teaser to compel you to give up some personal information. That information generally has to do with the following: Name, phone, email address, current "pre-qualification", time frame, size and price of different homes that you might be interested in and the area. Guess what happens next: You become a "lead".

Lead generation is (or should be) the largest investment of any real estate brokerage. It is prudent; however uncommon, for such brokerages to actually do the homework and determine what the return on investment (ROI) will be prior to making that investment in lead generation. Because this homework isn't normally done, the following generally takes place: The only qualifying factors that can possibly serve as qualifying metrics are the factors that those "leads" personally input when filling out their initial registration information. As you can probably see, there is an inherent skew if these metrics are used as part of a marketing presentation to you the seller.

The ability to qualify, and eventually close, that lead on something that they are ready, willing and able to purchase becomes entirely dependent on only a few factors; one being, that lead's own tenacity to purchase something despite the best efforts of an inexperienced agent with their own agenda. Another factor being the fact that some buyer agent still has to pair the listing with a qualified buyer.

Tell me if you have ever heard this: "Did you know that in some States it takes roughly 1500 hours of pre-license education to become a hair dresser, also in some states, it takes less than 200 hours of pre-license education to become a licensed real estate agent?" Who cares, right? The reason I bring this up is not infer that I may or may not be a smarter, more qualified real estate agent than someone else.

The reason I bring it up is to bring light to the current reality within the real estate system. Co-existing brokerages within a common market depend on cooperating with one another in order to get anything done. That means that any listing can be sold by any cooperating brokerage, regardless of who the listing agency happens to be. From that perspective, doesn't it seem alarming to entrust 7.5% to an agency that will actively depend on its direct (and equally as inept) competition to sell your home? Scary.

Obviously, you can see where I am going with this. When you consider the "time versus return" ratio involved in each side of the transaction, it becomes very clear that there is a lot of money to be made by listing your home. Conversely, and using the same ratio, the anguish and effort associated with qualifying a lead and getting them all the way to a closing doesn't seem to make much sense for a broker to focus many resources. But, that's what "buyer specialists" are for. These are real estate agents who legally, have to work under a broker (as do all agents).

This is important, because they are just sales people . . . and they work for the brokerage . . . just like any other situation. They do pay to play, so to speak, and this is how.

Brokers compensate their agents, in this case, the "buyer specialist". Selling-side and listing-side brokers are both compensated by the seller as defined by the terms negotiated within the listing agreement. The buyer agent's compensation is generally based upon their performance within the brokerage and paid from some sort of a split agreement stemming from the buyer side compensation of the accepted offer. That "buyer side compensation" comes from a home seller's original listing agreement that was discussed above.

A common example might be a "55% split". What that means is that if a home sells for $200,000, and the seller agreed to compensating the selling broker 3%, then, the lowly real estate agent—who got someone under contract and all the way to closing (a 40 day process)

is compensated an amount equal to $200,000 × .03 × .55 equaling roughly $3300 less any other in-house dues or admin/marketing fees. The remainder of the buyer side 3% compensation goes to the broker of the buyer agent. The broker easily justifies that compensation split under the premise of lead generation and support staff expense.

If that brokerage were also the listing agency, then there would be the selling side (listing) commission earned as well. I routinely see 7% total; so in this example, that 3% would be split between the agent and their broker, and the remaining 4% would go directly to the brokerage (Unless, of course the listing was the agent's own personal listing . . . which happens at times).

Generally speaking, individual agents shy away from the complexities of listing. They are simply frightened by the details associated with abstract work, repairs, etc. But once they do figure it out . . . The act of listing is either embraced or completely avoided.

There are also lots of other lines of income that are tacked on in the form of "Document Prep" or "Transaction Fees", all used to increase the margin . . . . and interestingly, most if not all of these are legally passed along to the seller's side of the HUD-1 settlement statement as some form of negotiated for buyer closing cost. It is a wonderful misconception in that we generally associate a buyer to be the one who is spending the money. As you can see, it is the seller who is doing the spending; the buyer is only taking out a loan and providing the brokerage a conduit to expense the seller.

Chapter 2

Buyer Agent Compensation and Motivation

I have found out that I am very effective on the phone, but deadly face-to-face. It isn't about ripping out client's eyeballs or tearing out throats . . . It is about rapport and relationship building, trust building, sounding brilliant and being very excited and sincere as quickly as this can all be established . . . and then helping that client to see that you are the best at what you do and that you are passionate about helping them to reach their goals. This is not a home buying or selling idea. It is about getting them to their ideal situation. This is "sales 101".

When shopping for a good buyer's agent, you may or may not encounter such a polished presentation. But, if you do, give them the opportunity to get through it. Just make sure that your agent is extremely knowledgeable about the systematic process and timelines involved. The perspective buyer's agent that you are interviewing will not like it when you make them clearly articulate this process to you and in a way that you understand. It doesn't matter though; they must demonstrate a solid understanding of these principles prior to doing you doing anything. I will go into that entire process as well as give you a few examples of some of my more effective closes.

Be sure that you understand that your agent's motivation has nothing to do with you. That isn't a bad thing at all because they are in business to make money as efficiently as possible. Their time is as valuable as yours, so use the agent's focus as a qualifying metric in your search for the right agent for you.

The agent is qualifying you as well. This is why you will almost always be asked, "Are you pre-qualified?" (This refers to being prequalified for a loan). This is their juvenile way qualifying a buyer and determining who is ready, willing and able. Don't be offended; you as the buyer have a large piece in this process. Do it before you even consider talking to an agent or a seller. You are getting ready to make one of the largest transactions in your life, so you should probably talk to a qualified, licensed mortgage lender in order to determine exactly what and how you can buy. I will go into the treatment of mortgage lenders in a moment, but first, let's continue to delve into a buyer's agent mindset.

Effective agents shouldn't default to a larger priced transaction . . . only the number of transactions in their pipeline, so let's look at that difference in real terms. What is the difference between a $200,000 sale and a $220,000 sale for an average buyer's agent? You will understand why I am defining this for you in a moment, but for now, bear with me.

A well-compensated (non-broker) buyer's agent will make approximately 1.7% of the gross sales price. That means that for $200k they will make $3400. For a $220k sale, they will make $3740, or a $340 difference. That means that they should have the same care and approach to the $75k deal as they do the $400k deal. The process is identical. If the agent is any good at all, they will have their systems in place and make the process feel as smooth as silk, regardless of the size of the transaction. Your expectations will have been managed and there will be no surprises; and not a lot of dialogues, outside of a possible twice-weekly check-in "hug" call.

Back to the example, it is quite normal to have a $20k swing in price during the negotiations of a transaction. This is important to consider in that the seller is almost always focused on price, while the buyer is focused on cost.

I want you to consider that based on these numbers, your buyer agent's advice for making a good offer has an effective compensation margin for them of $340. This equates to a night at the bar with several friends; which when balanced against the anxiety you will bear throughout the negotiation phase, isn't much. In those terms, their advice is really not worth much. Another consideration is that a difference of $20,000 in price when financed over 30 years at a fixed rate of 3.5% costs roughly $89 per month.

Is $89 per month worth $20k to you? It is to the seller, so you could just give it to them . . . and then ask for everything else, they will give it to you, do you know why? They have likely been told that these concessions have already been accounted for in the worse case scenario listing presentation they likely received.

OK, so if you offered $200k (instead of $220k) and are asking for $13.2k in concessions, the seller will see this and likely counter back with what they need to make it work. Again, you must consider the FACT that the seller has very likely rolled all of your closing costs to include a home warranty, a high repair cap, etc., which will equal as much as 6% gross sales price, or $13,200 . . . as well as any negative equity they may have. So, help "get them out of jail". If your buyer's agent fails to articulate this 5th grade math to you, run away.

Had that seller not been managed to expect this request at the outset, this may be too painful of a request to float by way of an offer. However, they won't be opposed to the idea of getting what they need to make it all "just work", which will hopefully prompt them to compose a seller's counter to the buyer's offer. Just remember, that's a good thing because 1: now you are having a conversation and 2: you already know what their counter will say before you have seen it. You will very likely get everything you asked for, and you will be paying (financing) a few thousand dollars less than what you would have in the first place.

What I am trying to articulate to you is that you can do this yourself if you choose to. If you do use an agent, make sure they completely understand these concepts. Further, the seller is only thinking about their net earnings. So if this makes sense to you, read on for some terms and concepts that you will need to be able to articulate when approaching a seller on your own; again, if you so choose to use a buyer's agent.

Remember, it isn't you the buyer, who is footing the buyer agent's cost . . . it is the seller. In this regard, it is actually better to use a buyer's agent that has a clue. Use them up; they will be happy that someone is talking to them. Leverage their professional insecurity to your benefit, so long as they can demonstrate these principles prior to you starting.

Chapter 3

A Thought on Lenders
(for Buyers)

Conventional banks are funny places. You stick in your money and it essentially becomes an idea. You are putting an organization in charge of managing your money, so why wouldn't they charge you for the facilitation of your assets.

If you want to open a checking account, you go to a bank whose main activity centers on the maintenance (and consequent multi-level billing) of those funds. Why then would you go to a bank (conventional lender), whose main focus is the consistent, gradual, persistent and predatory bilking of your checking and savings accounts when trying to find someone that can help you with mortgage lending?

All financial institutions have investors. Those investors have minimum requirements that must be met in order for a transaction's risk to be authorized. The management of that risk is commonly referred to as "overlays". If you have a lender that if primarily focused on mortgage lending, then their overlays will be much more timely and flexible in terms of dealing with your specific need and situation; or better, your priorities.

Those priorities (of yours) often entail not paying for closing, which the lender can sometimes mitigate with lender credit. Other priorities have to do with the amount of down payment that may be needed in the event a government-backed loan is used. Yet another consideration is the management of mortgage insurance.

Bottom line, conventional banks will generally treat your home purchase as if you are purchasing a used car. Also, in those conventional banking situations, those "loan officers" are not individually licensed. The bank holds the license and the "loan officers" all work under that bank's umbrella. There is an obvious disconnect between the loan officer (in that situation) and their access to the investor or their underwriters.

Wouldn't you rather deal with a lender that deals specifically with the type of transaction that you are trying to figure out? Wouldn't you rather deal with a licensed mortgage lender? Wouldn't you rather deal with a person that has exponentially more transactions and experience under their belt?

A lot of agents have non-official relationships with different mortgage lenders. If you ask any agent for a recommendation on whom to use as a mortgage lender, they will most definitely give you 1 or 2 options. They will give you these recommendations based on comfort level of reporting, getting information, simple things like the lender picking up their phone and being upfront with the situation, etc.

The industry is based on relationships and experience. A good lender/agent team is incredibly valuable and this will cause your transaction to look and feel insanely simple and without drama. At the end of the day, the lender that you use is your choice. You can shop around, but do so before you get into the offer/negotiation phase. I sometimes make a recommendation for a specific lender based on the buyer's priorities and personality type. For example, if the buyer is concerned about the expense associated with closing costs, I will try to find a lender that has a lender credit program.

I know what price point the buyer is looking at, so I just ask the prospective lender how much lender credit they could come up with if pushed. Then, I do a worst case scenario "net-sheet" for the buyer for that price point identifying highest case values for home-owners insurance and taxes (pre-paid buyer expenses) and figure out what the worst case scenario closing costs will be. After that, I subtract that lender credit amount offered from that lender from the "worse case" number I came up with.

When the buyer finds something to make an offer on, update the numbers and then offer the seller an offer with seller conceding a lower buyer closing cost value then they expected to concede. I am essentially leveraging the lender's "lender credit" into the buyer's offer.

Sometimes, I upset the lenders I work with because I will initially send the buyer to a bank and then tell them to, "Ask the lender for a fee sheet". (The biggest reason that I do this is because it isn't really that ethical to steer a perspective client to a single lender). Then, when they go to my preferred lender, they simply need to state: "Here you go, beat this", which almost always happens. That newly discovered savings is generally realized in up front overhead costs like transaction fees, origination fees, etc.; but not interest rates, those are based on your credit history.

Prior to submitting an offer, the buyer will need to obtain a Conditional Loan Approval from a valid lending institution. It is during the qualification phase that the lender will assist the buyer in determining the maximum buyer's purchasing power. It is not a guarantee that a loan will be given; however, it does check your credit worthiness and known history. The Buyer or Seller should not confuse this with a Final Loan Commitment that is not obtained until prior to closing to ensure all of the Buyer's financials are considered.

Bottom line, money is like milk. It doesn't matter if you go to Wal-Mart or the corner store . . . . milk is milk, it doesn't matter where you buy it. How much do you want to pay for it? Do you mind if it smells bad in the store or if it's out of the way? That's all up to you; generally speaking though, just stay away from conventional banks if you are trying to buy a house. They generally embrace a "shove the square into the circle" mentality and completely overcharge you by using a flat fee approach for billing transactions. They are just not able to provide the flexibility that you will need in order to maximize upon your priorities.

Another thought, a good rule of thumb is that the lower the mortgage costs the higher the interest rate will be. Whomever you decide to use, ask for the fee sheet or a "good faith estimate" (GFE) and do a comparison. Just understand that most lenders are not required to prepare a GFE unless you actually apply for a loan with them, but many more times than not, they will prepare a good estimate that will likely confirm what your buyer's agent has already shared with you.

Chapter 4

The Process

The Offer. Negotiations to purchase a home technically begin when the Buyer makes a written offer to purchase the Seller's home. The Seller may accept, reject, or make a counteroffer to the Buyer's offer. The offer may go back and forth until both parties have agreed to all terms in writing, and the document has been delivered to both Buyer and Seller (or their Broker as authorized). At this point, the offer becomes a contract (See appendix 1 for a complete example of a Residential Contract of Sale of Real Estate). After completion of the book, you must read through that document in its entirety; it is only then that you will see and understand how all of this fits together.

There are many other preparatory issues that need to be identified prior to even getting to the formulation of an offer. Every single one of those preparatory issues have to do with you being able to voice exactly what your priorities are and having those considerations actually be heard by a real estate agent.

During the Offer and Counter process, the listing broker (if one is used, the listing broker must adhere to this rule) is required by the law (depending on the State) to continue presenting all offers to the Seller up until the time the Seller accepts an offer in writing. Further, during the offer/counteroffer process, the Seller may withdraw the Seller's counteroffer and accept another contract if the Seller's counter has not been accepted and signed by the Buyer and delivered back to the Seller (or if authorized, the listing broker).

Likewise, Buyer may withdraw Buyer's offer and purchase a different property if the Buyer's offer has not been accepted and signed by the Seller and delivered back to the Buyer, (or if authorized, the selling broker). All items of a contract are negotiable between the Buyer and Seller.

None of this says that you must use a broker for listing or for selling; these limitations are set forth for the protection and good of the buyer and the seller when represented by a respectively interested set of third parties.

Even within these few paragraphs, you can see how easily the buyer/seller negotiation process can be confounded. I have tried thus far to identify the additive nature of using a broker or real estate agent in representing an individual's real estate needs; however, "additive" does not mean essential. In a way, you can easily see how valuable an experienced buyer's agent can be. The fact remains that it is difficult to find one that will spend the hours needed to guide you through this minefield.

At this point, if it seems to be too much, stop reading, but if you want to see the rest of what you don't necessarily need a licensed agent or broker to do, please continue reading.

The Contract consists of the contract form and any related addenda and/or attachments. Once signed by both the Buyer and Seller, the contract is valid and binding upon each party — if either party does not understand the contract, the party should seek advice from an attorney.

Each party, both Buyer and Seller, should read the entire contract and related addenda and attachments. The Contract shall be executed by original signatures of the parties or by signatures as reflected on separate identical Contract counterparts (scanned copies, faxes, etc.).

Within the contract, there should be a discussion of the Legal Description. This should contain the legal and physical property address. The contract, unless altered, shall include all surface rights and appurtenances, but generally not the mineral rights.

The earnest money should be identified within the contract as well. An earnest money deposit of 1-1.5% or less is customary in most markets. The earnest money deposit is required in situations where a home is listed and marketed.

The Earnest money serves as a security for the seller as a possible compensation for the time that the seller has taken their home off the market in the event that contract breaks (subject to minimum timelines). Those funds are deposited into an appropriate third party escrow account must be exchanged from the buyer to the seller (or seller's appointed brokerage as appropriate) upon a fully executed and delivered contract.

The purchase price and source of those funds are identified as well. The contract is designated for a cash transaction unless a Financing Supplemental Agreement is attached (i.e., FHA, VA, and Conventional). That supplemental shares many of the same elements as the contract, but also specifies responsibility of common appraisal related requirements.

The offer will likely get kicked back and forth in the offer, counter, buyer counter-offer phase. One thing that I like to do for the buyer, but not necessarily for the buyer's knowledge, is simply pull the tax records on whatever home the buyer is interested in. Anyone can do this, and it is almost scary how quickly you can reverse engineer the seller's position and offering price point.

Ask your buyer agent to pull the tax record. Look at when the home was purchased, by whom and for how much. Then, do an Internet search for the average mortgage interest rate that was in effect during that month and year. Depending on the age of the owner/seller, you will also have some good insight into which loan family was used (VA, FHA, Conventional). Paying attention to the year of purchase will also provide some gradient resolution to the situation you are looking at.

For example, if the loan was an FHA, subtract 3.5% (their down payment) from the purchase price and then simply run a monthly amortization table starting at the purchase month. Follow the table down to today's date and take note of the principle balance.

This is only a worse case estimate, but I'll bet you that if you take that principle balance number corresponding to the current month and year and multiply that by 1.12 (Remember that 12.2% in chapter 1?), 9 times out of 10, you will be looking at the seller's asking price.

By doing this, I can help the buyer understand that the seller is not out to rip them off; but that the seller is simply looking for someone to cooperate with them in helping them get out of the financial responsibility of maintaining that home. Only after doing this homework will I have a discussion with the buyer as to what I think would be a good offer.

In my practice, I act as a transaction broker (a glorified assistant or advisor). That means that I can't be held responsible for my client's actions, and vice versa. I hope to simply provide a background of possibilities for the buyer to consider thus helping them come to a clear understanding of the situation so that they can make their own informed decision. When advising the buyer on a possible way used to discover the seller's "magic number" you may hear something to the following.

"Bla bla bla" . . . math . . . "bla bla bla" . . . principle balance . . . 12% . . . BAM! Look at that". Then ask the buyer if they would like to figure out exactly what the seller's "number" is. Of course, the buyer says, "yes". So I say something to the effect of, "you might consider offering them what you believe their principle balance to be, and then simply ask for all of the concessions that you have identified as priorities, i.e., buyer closing, home warranty, high repair caps . . . etc." I continue, "The seller is psychologically attached to their "get out of jail" number.

I am repeating myself here, but regardless of what ever concession you are asking for, and so long as that number is associated with the concessions that you are seeking, the seller will almost always counter back giving you everything that you asked for while communicating exactly what their number (purchase price) has to be. Either-way, you will save a few thousand dollars in closing expenses or purchase price, let's give it a shot . . . if you don't ASK, you will never GET, especially if you are dealing with an unprepared seller or seller's agent.

Did you see what just happened? I just got you to make an offer that is within striking distance, which WILL generate a counter offer. This is good, because that leaves you, the buyer feel as if you are in control. What is interesting is the fact that when that counter comes back, I have already managed your expectations by making you analyze the differences between cost and price motivation and the resulting strength leveraged by financing. Remember how much $20,000 will cost you? In this instance, it only cost you a little more than $13k. If you are wondering, no, I have never sold cars.

At this point, you likely have an accepted offer. This is referred to as being "under contract". As soon as that happens, you the buyer will see a few things happen. First, your earnest money will be deposited into an escrow account. Second, your agent will (should) give you a few recommendations on home inspectors in your area. You will have to pay the inspector out of pocket because they are working for you. Don't worry though; these inspections are generally very inexpensive considering the size of the purchase that you are considering.

Once the inspection takes place, you will receive their report, and your buyer's agent will go over the information with you. The inspection report is not an estimate, but is only a good third party, trained look at what the property is or isn't. Not everything has to be fixed, but this is where some of these things can be addressed to the seller.

If you remember in the initial offer, there was mention of a "repair cap". This is where the repair cap comes into play. If after your initial walk through, you and your agent can pretty quickly estimate how much money will be needed to get the place up to a livable condition. Basically, the worse the condition, the higher the repair cap.

So, with the inspection report in hand, your buyer agent will formalize a list of concerns sometimes referred to as a Treatment, Replacement, Repair request. The items of concern should be listed in a prioritized order on that sheet and given to the buyer for acknowledgement.

Acknowledgement does not mean consent to repair, but does mean that your "time period" has effectively ended. This is big, because there is normally a period of time after the offer goes "under contract" that the buyer can back out with out penalty and still receive their earnest money back with no questions. The other consideration is that the cost of the repairs requested will have to fall beneath that prior agreed upon repair cap.

There are opportunities to further renegotiate that number, but it isn't common. If repairs can't be completed prior to closing, it is normal to have the cost of that repair escrowed and paid upon closing.

While all this is going on, the buyer will also meet with their lender to get all required loan application and supporting documents. This is also when the lender will order the appraisal. When the appraisal is ordered, there is a fee charged by the lender to the buyer. This fee is outside of closing and is for the bank to determine the ability of the home to prove and maintain its market value. The fee is small, but worth it. Think of it like this, your home inspection is to you as the appraisal is to the bank.

The appraisal will take time to get "picked up" by an appraiser, and then another few days to actually get done. It will be delivered to the lender upon its completion. If there are any repairs that are required to be made, the seller is generally required to make those repairs prior to close.

In the offer, there is also a repair cap for appraisal-required repairs. This is treated much the same as the TRR cap, but in some instance, and as directed by what type of financing the buyer is using; those costs will have to be absorbed by the seller anyway.

Once the appraisal comes back, the closing coordinator with and the listing agent, buyer and seller respectively, will begin their part. The listing agent will order the release of the abstract from where ever it is being stored and the buyer side closing coordinator will request that a title company start the gap search and bring the title documentation up to date for eventual addition to the abstract. The title/abstract pieces take about a week and occur after the appraisal. These are going concurrently to the underwriting that is going on with the lender.

Underwriting is the process where lender staff reviews requirements of the type of loan and work to minimize risk within the guidelines of their investors. It is the underwriter who ultimately gives the loan approval based on the condition of the home as well as the credit worthiness of the buyer.

During this time, the title company or closing company is getting the abstract/title/attorney opinion updated and your lender is working concurrently to get you a confirmation to close. Maybe a day prior to that, you will receive a copy of the settlement statement, which was prepared by the lender and the title agency. It is the title agency that acts as the escrow manager and pays out only after all requirements have been contractually met.

That's a lot of stuff, right? Well, maybe so, but if you look at it, who is doing the lion's share of work in this situation? It isn't the listing agent. More like it is everyone except for the listing agent. Do you remember the normal listing/buying commission negotiated during the listing agreement? Was it 4% listing and 3% buying? That said; are you starting to get the picture of where you can save money when selling a home?

People don't sell houses . . . they sell homes their motivation to sell has to do with up sizing, downsizing, moving, or simply stopping the financial bleeding. Buyers buy for the same reason that sellers sell; none of it is about money, it's about transference. Alternatively, brokers list houses to make money. For all the effort that goes into the 40-day (minimum) emotional nightmare of relationship building, motivating, qualifying, managing expectations and then getting them all the way to the closing table . . . all for 1.7% of that gross sales price . . . it doesn't make sense to not disclose how this actually goes. If you knew this stuff before you came to me, the buyer's agent . . . your transaction would take less than a month, and we could both focus on bigger and better things.

Just for perspective, your $220k deal works out to be a $3740 payout upon closing for the buyer's agent that you have "hired". Divide that $3740 by 40 days (time it takes from offer to closing), and then again by 1/2 an hour per day (phone calls, coordination, document preparation and movement, etc.) averages out to about $187/hour.

I can tell you that I am worth every penny, and you should agree with me; do you know why? It is because the seller that just sold your house to you is paying me that $187/hour, not you. So, if you think about it and I am your agent, I am leveraging your interests: i.e., protecting your interests and fighting to minimize your costs, in order to take advantage of the seller's position. Everything about the system is about ripping the eyeballs out of the seller's head.

So who cares, right? Why do you suppose that something like this would be useful to both the homebuyer and the home seller? If you think about it, that compensation given to the buy-side agent is rational. I mean there is a lot of stuff that you have to do in terms of coordination, scheduling, document preparation; always being there on demand for the buyer's questions. On the other hand, the seller side compensation really is not justified in terms of effort given for money spent by you the seller.

This idea is commonly refer to this factor as "touch time". I spoke about this earlier, but want to revisit the idea just because it means much in terms of dollars. I am going to go start to finish through both sides of a possible transaction, starting with the seller (listing side) and illustrate the costs involved.

Not dealing with "touch time" I need to breakdown the "upfront money" needed to get through this phase. It is minimal and generally follows this example:

- Your earnest money will need accompany your offer in the form of a personal check. It will be between .5 and 1% of the offer price.
- Upon acceptance of your offer you will need to pay a home inspector to come and do a home inspection on your behalf. This amount is relative to your area. These are relatively inexpensive.
- After the inspection has come back "good", you will be asked by your lender to pay for an appraisal. I estimate between $400 and $500.
- If you have opted to do any sort of down-payment to accompany your financing (i.e., you took a conventional or an FHA loan), your lender will ask you for those funds during the underwriting phase (or at least proof of them)
- Any closing costs identified by your lender, but you will have known about this well in advance (It would have been identified during the negotiation/offer phase).

Chapter 5

The Listing Appointment
(you are the Seller now)

You decide you need to move or sell your house for some reason. You are not sure where to start, so you begin looking up how to do it yourself; if at very least, just for the information. You ask around for some sort of experiential feedback and eventually go so far as to actually call a real estate brokerage and set up an appointment for you to get some information on listing your home.

Depending on the agency, there should be a representative that will initially field your call. They will not talk to you about price, but will ask as many questions as needed in order to give someone else down the line (a listing agent) an opportunity to develop a very quick rapport with you during an in-office meeting that you are getting ready to be asked to come to. You get off the phone feeling good because you get the sense that you have finally found someone who will listen to you because they have made you feel very comfortable.

Some of the questions asked, but not emphasized are: "So, is your home paid off?" Generally, this will make you feel good, as it was just communicated to you that you obviously have your finances in order and "of course you would have your home paid off". The fact is, the representative already understands the reality that you don't and has just made you feel very comfortable . . . so much so that you immediately tell that representative what your principle balance is on your mortgage(s).

You make an appointment, hang up, and the rep then hits the county tax assessors' database and looks at what the baseline information is concerning your property. This is also done to confirm that we are actually talking to the party that has the authority to sell the home. We look at things like square footage, how many rooms and bathrooms, what type of garage, lot size, age, effective tax rate; but most importantly, the location.

Based on that, the agency does a quick look at everything that has been sold over the last 2-3 years in the area, as well as everything that has been listed, taken off the market, or didn't sell. We also figure in the existing inventory that is in direct competition with your home, and the life expectancy of that inventory.

That means that if you have 10 or so months of inventory on the market in that price range, you will have to price your home below the average (use square footage/price ratio for an easy look) that is currently being demonstrated in your market. We don't care about doing a comparative market analysis, because we are not doing an appraisal. We are preparing the numbers needed to illustrate to you the actual high and low market boundaries your within your home's market. Then, based on a walk through, your home's condition, your motivation to sell, we can come to a pretty good conclusion on exactly where to "place your home within the market".

Here are some other things to consider when you hear the "CMA pitch" or the "deep analysis activities".

- Property condition, has it been staged properly, was there a loss of job, is it under priced?
- Is the interior dated?
- Has the property been inherited by an ineffectual or incompetent family member?

- Is the seller extremely motivated by divorce or other factors?
- Have they moved?
- Is the house ugly from the road?

This is a hat to wear by both the buyer and the seller . . . . "Who cares", Stuff sells for more and later if prepared and faster and for less if unprepared. If a realtor* comes to you and uses the language of "CMA", I'd be sure to ask questions that have to do with anything that I have referenced in this paragraph alone.

Just ask, "What's the story? Why?" CMAs are manipulated and if you buy into them, so shall will you be. Look at the numbers that are supportive and justify such things and the effective tax rate within that neighborhood. Make them do the math. If they can't, fire them on the spot and then send them a bill for wasting your time with their unpreparedness and stupidity.

If you are able to find an agent that seems to be knowledgeable, make an appointment. You will go in for your sit-down appointment with them. At that point, they will go through all of their various disclosures, as well as all of the marketing tools that are used by the company. Then, they will likely start talking about all of the metrics that the company's repeatable results are based upon.

This is the part where you are given an "upsell". It is at this point that you will be presented with other opportunities to talk about different products and programs that will enhance your home's "sell-ability"; i.e., getting a pre-inspection done, staging, cleaning, paint and other cosmetics (landscaping). These are all that you will pay for if you so choose. Then, if that agent has demonstrated himself or herself to be an expert, they will likely begin with the presentation of the listing agreement.

Have you noticed that you haven't even really talked price yet? You haven't because right now you are being lulled into a posture of cooperative behavior and responsibility. That simply means that you will begin seeing the positive effects of what will happen if you listen to and comply with the advice that this person is telling you.

There is a very essential cooperative action that must take place. You must be made feel as if you are in charge and making the decisions. That's why, up until now, you have been "pitched" several different opportunities to likely enhance your home listing experience. Really, depending on your reaction to these things and your personality type, things will take a few different paths at this point. Either-way, the name of the game now is to give you the pain element of the pleasure-pain-pleasure sandwich that you are eating and don't even know it.

Your listing agent will ask you, "If you had to pick a number right now, what would you like to see your home sell for?" If you don't answer it, he or she would simply re-frame the question and ask you again. Eventually, you will give them your "number".

This is the place where different agencies depart in their methodology. Many times, and in order to get the deal, lesser listing agents would simply say, "That's completely do-able, sign here and let's get it done". The sad part is, that agent has likely done no analysis whatsoever on the current market and couldn't help advise you to do the right thing for you if they tried.

Anyway, this is where your listing agent would introduce you to a high and a low number and then demonstrate why based on historical sales data in that area.

You are reasonable, and you have been agreeable and rational up to this point, and you are not going to disagree with hard fact; therefore, you will be forced to pick a number that is within the bracket. Interestingly, even if you voice price objections, the same sort of "cost over time" analysis will be presented you, which was used against a buyer when trying to get them to spend an additional $10-20k.

You say "ok", and then you are introduced to the listing agreement. You will likely be shown and explained the numbers if takes for the listing side commission as well as the selling side commission.

Your listing agent will not want to negotiate their listing side commission, but will be very happy to negotiate the selling side of your listing arrangement. Remember, they will not be trying to sell your home . . . that takes too much time; they are only interested in listing your home.

Fun fact re-visited . . . . around 70% of all real estate transactions are sold by a different agent then the one who listed it. So, from the listing agent's perspective, it doesn't make good financial sense or management of time to put any more effort than is needed into the deal.

Anyway, you agree to a 3-4% commission on the listing side probably a 3% selling side. Those numbers will not change and are now part of a contract between you and that agency. Further, look for a transaction fee as well as the amount needed to break your listing agreement.

I have seen transaction fees in the amount of $700 and "break agreement" fees up to $1500. These are sold to you as an evidence of proven self-worth of that agency and what they will do for you. The question is: What do they actually do for you?

After your agreement is signed, your home specs (that you provided) are indicated on a multi-listing system (MLS) sheet; i.e., how many rooms, etc. The photos that the agency sends someone out to get are then organized and uploaded. Then, a little block called "IDX" is checked. IDX is an acronym for "Internet Data Exchange".

IDX references the transfer of MLS data, from the MLS Board to Realtor websites. Obviously, that broker/agency that you just listed with has a relationship with that MLS board in that they are a member and pay dues. This is important to realize in that those dues pay for IDX transfers out to the Internet as well as pay the board to act as a disinterested third party for arbitration in the event that something shady goes down (between the agencies involved in the transaction, not necessarily for your behalf).

I am talking this down to identify the fact that there is cost involved in having a membership to that market's board or Realtors*. It also costs (generally on an hourly basis) to have an experienced individual being able initially organize and upload your listing, as well as maintain any updates that are needed as time goes on.

Depending on the set up of that listing agency, either the listing agent or the MLS coordinator will be the individual assisting in the negotiations of your listing should an offer come in. We will get into that dynamic a bit later. Right now, I want to focus primarily on the justification of 3-4% commission to your listing agency in consideration of what really takes place after your home is listed. Ask the question, how is that 3-4% really earned?

The next thing that takes place is a lock box (generally associated with the local MLS) and a sign is stuck in your yard. Now people can drive by, or your home will pop up on any number of third party internet sites that make their money from buyers agents putting their photos and bios all over them for a specific market.

Then, you just wait. Depending on the inventory (competition), how nice or how much of a dump your home is, and where it is priced will directly affect whether or not someone makes an offer on your home.

The average sold time might be anywhere from 45 days to 4-5 months. During that time, there will be the initial agreement meeting, as well as 1 or 2 phone calls or emails per month and then upon an offer, there will be some negotiation and a signature needed in order to order an abstract. That is pretty limited "touch time" when considering that your $200,000 home that will eventually sell will pay that brokerage an astounding $4000 for roughly 5 hours total work throughout the life of your listing agreement.

Another misconception within the industry is how the real estate agency does all of the work required in the areas is title, abstract, appraisal, lending and attorney opinion. These external systems are not built in; they are referred out by the agency as a listing comes under contract that you pay for as necessary.

The above example is based on a company centric organization where taking listings is the primary focus. This would imply that it is very well organized with specific roles carried out by specific individuals within that organization. Sadly, this example is the best-case scenario in that most agencies bring on agents, and then simply hire an office manager.

To stay above water, those types of brokerages simply tax their sales associates in some manner or another just as a hair salon might charge "stall rent". What that means is that the same 4 hours of work that was discussed above is now going to be left to a single person who is either not experienced, or at very least, not very focused on your home.

The alarming part is that the single agent situations, when compared to the listing centric company model, all bear the same fruit; only the single agent model will be an extremely more painful experience as they are generally not backed with the necessary resources, time or simple know-how that the counterpart agency has to offer.

While it would seem that the single person would be a better financial choice as the time ratio would indicate (more touch time), the reality is simply that the increased "touches" will be due to that agent's ineffectiveness or inefficiency. Another consideration is experience. A single agent will not have the sheer number of "at bats" that the company model will.

There are obvious pros and cons within this larger con; but please remember to ask yourself, "Are the things that have been mentioned here really that difficult? Are these things really worth $4000 worth of equity that you have built up over the last several years?" No, obviously not, but how do I do it then?

Chapter 6

The "sale assist" approach
(not popular among listing agencies)

Ok, this is the hard part; I am going to demonstrate first what NOT to do. The ideas below will be very confrontational to anyone; especially considering you are giving them the opportunity to "pitch" to you. Remember, their goal is NOT to sell your house; their goal is to get a listing agreement with you so that you can pay them for the effort (however minimal) involved in listing your home.

Obviously, nothing really happens until something sells, but consider that if 20% of a listing agency's inventory sells within the 1st two months of it being listed, it seems to make sense that listing agents would seek to attack every opportunity to secure a listing. They are effectively "putting hay in the barn".

Generally speaking, (you can double check with the National Association of Realtors, or NAR) every home that is listed has a 50-90% chance of selling. Based on that, your listing agent/broker will simply look at the amount of inventory (normally described in months at different price points), and do the simple math. They are looking at the number of listings that must be taken on a monthly basis in order to maintain that company's financial goals. You are a number, no offense.

When you face that listing agent, just tell them: "Before you start, I want you to know that I really value your time, so this is what I am willing to offer you . . ."

"I want to offer you a buyer side compensation of 3% (or whatever the prevailing percentage for buy-side commission in your market). In order to maximize this offer for you, I'd like to offer you a chance to earn more for your agency, or whoever sells it, a bonus of 0.5% of gross sales price.

If you want, I will list my home with you for 1%; which, I believe to be fair considering that you have to pay staff for data entry, signage, photos, and membership fees to our market's multiple listing service."

"I want you to know that I am prepared to pay for a home warranty, and likely, some of the buyer closing costs if need be. If you take all of that out of my sale price of $200,000, which leaves me with $9000 being paid in real estate commissions, as well as a worst case scenario of being asked for an additional $3500-$4000 in buyer closing costs."

What they know is the fact that, "IDX" will systematically take care of pushing your listing out to all of the various searchable real estate websites out there. Follow up again with this, "but again, in order to focus on our local market, I know that a buyer's agent will be working their tail off for that extra .5% bump; and to make things easier on you, I have decided also to provide a pre-inspection report and will have my home professionally staged."

At this point, they will probably focus on the number that you just mentioned: $200,000. Ask them to run a scatter gram of all of the listings and what happened to them over the last 3 years. Then ask for an inventory report so they can demonstrate the competition that is out there that you will have to price beneath. Whatever the price point they counter with, just keep the same ratio values in place.

Chances are, your listing agent will not have the first idea about any of this . . . that's fine. Bottom line, you know how much you need to sell for in order to meet your priorities as well as take care of the overhead that we just demonstrated.

Your listing agent will not be pleased if you take this approach, but the name of the game is not appeasing an agent whose only goal is to secure a listing agreement. If forced to provide proof of the metrics that have (or will be) cited throughout the listing presentation, the chances are very good that you will never see them.

Just call a small broker, promise them a referral back and ask them to list your house for 1%. Tell them that you will get a pre-inspection, pay for a home warranty and buyer closing costs not to include buyer's pre-paids (their insurance and taxes that they will have to escrow for the first year of their mortgage. Also tell them that you want to put a 3% buyer side compensation and a small bonus, i.e., 0.25-0.5% of sales price.

They will very likely agree to it because they will get credit for the unit that they just listed and got sold. They will also get credit for moving your listing faster than the market average "Days on Market". They will earn your business and treat you with respect. You will be a joy for them to pick up the phone for when you call, because you know what you are doing; and not incessantly asking, "Why?"

OK, so now you have the broad terms of what is needed in order to save yourself a lot of money, but what are all those other things you were talking about? What is a pre-inspection? What is staging? What are pre-paids? What are buyer-closing costs? What is a home warranty? Why shouldn't I care what my past appraisal says my home is worth? Before you get that far, I want you to be thinking about how you can get that other 1% back and not use a listing agent at all. Before we can do that, there are some ideas that you must be familiar with.

Chapter 7

Staging and the Principles of Marketing

"Did you know that vacant homes consistently receive 15-20% less than market value?" "Did you know that at least 90% of ALL buyers absolutely can not visualize empty space?" Did you know that depending on your market, you might also be able to realize (accept) an offer up to 6% above list price if your home is staged?

Depending on your market, you might see that 65% of all homes that have been staged will receive an accepted offer within 30 days. You can easily say the same thing for 90% of all home sellers receiving an acceptable offer within 90 days. Best of all, depending on how much you spent on your staging experience, your return on investment (for staging) could be as much as 500% (if you figure the gross sales price of your home . . . are you kidding me?) That said, any sophomoric understanding of general marketing has to do with the following concepts: Place, Price, its Promotion and the Product itself.

Anyway, staging is important. It has nothing to do with HGTV, nor does it require you to spend a small fortune, upfront, on having some "professional staging advisor" come in to your home and tell you the following: Depersonalize, de-clutter, purpose the space . . . and then ask you to simply put it all in storage and then give you a budget for them to go to a furniture store and rent a bunch of nonsense for 3-4 months.

Just make it clean. Make it feel like a hotel, warm and purposed. It is not home decorating or about identifying your preferences concerning color and style. Home decorating is about personalization;

while conversely, staging is about de-personalization. You are setting out only to provide a minimal representation of a purpose for a given space. Think of it like this:

I am a hobbyist jazz musician. This euphemism may resonate with your or may not, but regardless, please bear with me. If you ever get the opportunity to listen to a small jazz group, say a 4 or a 5-piece band, you will see and hear them all participating in a mutual contribution to the same song. Now, imagine all of the musicians except one stopping playing, while the one continues on as if the others never quit.

You will be initially taken by the abstract and singular identification and demonstration of that musician's melodic and harmonic understanding of the song, as well as that musician's own virtuosity. That musician is playing to the reality of the chosen time, tempo and tone center that all musicians started with. The more interesting thing is what your ears are doing.

Despite the fact that you can no longer hear the drummer, the upright bass player, the pianist or the guitarist, you can mentally still hear the "comping" that those instruments would be doing if they were still playing. Your ear is filling in the spaces just as do your eyes when you walk into a purposed space. You begin to fill in up with your ideas of what is correct; thus, you are already starting to move in.

Location is a rather important factor to consider when either purchasing or selling your home. Real estate is distinguishable from tangible property because real estate is non-movable. How many external factors are there that can negatively or positively enhance the price point of the subject property? Is there a possibly high population of sexual offenders registered within the neighborhood? Is the property backed up against a railway? What is the proximity to your prospective purchase of overlooking neighbors?

An interesting corollary to location is price. You must consider that similarly built homes will have been built in common areas and according to specified code as directed by the corresponding city planner. What this means is that similar homes exist in immediate proximity to the subject property; so similar in fact, that these same homes will eventually be used as comparable properties when valuing the subject home for an appraisal, should it get that far.

This fact is something that you must consider when a listing agent comes to you and starts using words like "comparable market analysis". It simply does not make sense to use this approach when valuing your home in terms of the very market that is aching to reject your listing. Similar age, similar square footage, similar presentation, etc., these ideas can be easily expressed within a common ratio, and should be. Other things that must be considered are negative impacts to the subject property's market. How many foreclosures have there been? What is the current inventory? Have you effectively weighed these considerations when coming to the appropriate price point for placement of your home within the market affecting your home?

Marketing has been covered pretty well within the discussion of the concept of "IDX". Not to be pejorative, but again, please don't offer a response to the agent who offers anything other than volume, experience and numbers. Effective agencies are doing something right, otherwise they would no longer be in business; and you should listen. To some extent, those agencies should also be leveraged for your benefit. It is no secret that YAHOO, BING, Google, trulia, Zillow.com, etc., all represent the bulk of how roughly 99% of all homebuyers search (either initially or later for confirmation after initially meeting with an agent) for their home.

Don't get lulled into the following idea: If you have a brokerage with 1,000 signs all over town, and 50 billboards as well as a healthy local television presence; chances are better that if you list with them, your home will have the opportunity to be sold quicker . . . but how much quicker, and exactly what are the metrics that are being used to support their claims? You must remember that if someone, much like yourself, wants to list their home, they will go to the loudest listing presence. The thing to remember is that any buyer out there will likely follow the same line of thinking.

Your home, if listed, will have just as much visibility as all of the others; regardless of who lists it. One thing that you are up against, and is a reality in most major franchised brokerages, is the fact that if a buyer's agent sells a home that is not one of their brokerage's listings, then that buyer's agent is then taxed in that their internal compensation is significantly reduced; i.e., 75% down to 40% of 3% of the sales price.

The only thing that you can do in order to combat this situation is to put a bonus on top of your listing in order to make your $60,000 home compensate to the buyer side compensation as if it were a $100,000 purchase. Another option would be to put a higher buyer side compensation in your listing agreement as well as your bonus; i.e., 3.5% vs. 3%. That extra 0.5% will be a financial "bump" that will be realized and appreciated by every brokerage in the market.

The bottom line, "price" is not the only element of competition when trying to sell your home. The aspect of internal compensatory pressure (to sell in-house listings) is also a huge factor. This is an unfortunate truth and an internal control that is also very unfortunately used as policy by many brokerages. I can say that I have been on the opposite side of this very concept, and it is ugly; but under no circumstance will you, the buyer, ever be privy to the elements of having to deal with such things that are taking place on your behalf.

Steering in this sense is not steering in terms of general real estate dealings. Steering generally refers to the practice in which real estate professionals guide clients to or away from certain neighborhoods based upon race. The type of "steering" that I am referring to has to do with a brokerage prioritizing their own inventory above other existing inventory. This is normally done in an effort (from that brokerage) to gain both sides of the compensation agreement.

Now, let's talk about the product. This applies to both the buyer and the seller. If you are a buyer, please take note of the effort demonstrated by the seller in these areas. What it means to you is the deal will go well because the seller was educated; don't think of it as someone trying to misrepresent what it is they are trying to sell.

If you are a family person, where is it in your home that you spend most of your time together as a family: The kitchen, right? Please remember, you will not realize a dollar for dollar return on any upgrades that you wish to dive into; but there is an appropriate approach that will be useful in terms of maximizing the "wow factor", especially when on a budget.

Kitchens

I started with the kitchen because it is the easiest return on investment to achieve. At a minimum, this should be done prior to even considering staging or setting listing appointments. These ideas are based on going through hundreds of homes and trying to help the seller understand that their "good enough" will be greeted with a very cold "next" from any perspective buyer. Here are some basics.

Be sure that you have complimentary colors if you are using tile backsplashes, etc. Also, prior to ripping the old cabinetry off the walls, try first to strip and refinish them and then purchase new hardware. At the time of this writing, brushed nickel seems to be en vogue; whatever you use, make sure it matches throughout.

Ceramic flooring is not that expensive either, it just takes a few minutes to figure out what you are doing, and then you can change and upgrade the entire character of the space. If you don't know how to do it, go to your local DIY store and buy a book and read about it. You would be amazed at what you are capable of doing, and doing very well. At most, you will have to purchase a ceramic wet saw for less than $100 and materials. Use common sense and make it beautiful.

Your appliances must match. No one cares if they are not brand new, but make them all the same color or motif, and brand. If the appliance is built in somehow, remember that you can switch the face plating for less money. Spend an extra little bit on attractive fixtures, and when you do; make sure that you maintain that motif throughout the vision line (unobstructed line of sight from one end of your home to another). Light fixtures and good lighting are the best return on investment there is.

Countertops should have a "wow-factor". Instead of purchasing granite or whatever other hyper expensive fad may be persisting, consider using an offset compliment ceramic tile layout. This will easily cost 80% less than if you were to purchase a granite slab. Just take your time; the results will be astounding.

Bathrooms

If you have more than one bathroom that needs attention, primarily focus on whichever is associated with the master bedroom. That said; your bathtub doesn't necessarily need to be ripped out and replaced with some claw foot work of art. With grimy, disgusting, stained, old tubs, the key to success is careful preparation.

These kits generally consist of some sort of acid bath, a wash, some very fine steel wool and some sort of epoxy. This is a 3-day process that will cost less than $25, versus you buying a new tub, new plumbing, new tile and sheet rock, new paint, new fixtures, etc. If you are dealing with a one-piece fiberglass shower/pan or shower tub combo, then yes . . . tear it out. They are unsightly and scream: "I am a cheap piece of crap". A new tub isn't really that expensive and will fit in the space (they all generally do), and then just tile up the walls with some pretty 4x4 ceramic tile.

Update all the faucets as well. Stay away from gold finish, but most importantly; make it match throughout the effort of that bathroom.

Dump the commode and get a new ring seal, new braided stainless lines, seat and lid (preferably with hardware that is the same color as the other hardware in the bathroom). The same ideas apply as in the kitchen; however, the price for a much smaller piece of granite won't be that expensive as compared to a kitchen counter. Stay away from surfaces that are too porous, or just take it all out, re-tile the floor and get a pedestal. That option is nice in that it opens up the space for a much cleaner look. Let the buyer figure out where to hide all of their bathroom junk after they buy the house.

Curb Appeal

Drive-by buyers are buyers that are in the market right now, and would buy right now if someone would just answer the phone when they dial the information number and then are prompted to "dial 1 for the most up to date purchase price" because of "ever changing" or "an extremely fast" market . . . such a line of crap.

Anyway, We know that the buyer likes that area because they are driving around in that area. We also know that somehow, something about that house has caught their eye and has urged them to commit to showing that they are interested and making a call. What do you suppose it was that caused them to open themselves up to attack like that?

Are the lines between the paths and the vegetation well defined? Is everything neat? Where is the focal point of your eye-line from the road? From the road, does the focal point ask you to look at the door, to come into the home? How is the roofline? Do overgrown trees distort it? You might even consider tree based house lighting. The effect is magnificent at night. Does your lawn look as if it were something personally manicured by Calvin Cordozar Broadus, Jr? (That's Snoop dogg to the rest of you.)

Chapter 8

The Pre-Inspection

Imagine listing your home, either my way or pay more for the same effort. Then you get through the offer negotiation phase and enter into the inspection phase. Up to this point, you as the seller have become very knowledgeable about everything within your home because you have been living there for several years. The fact is you have become accustomed to the squeaky floors, the sticky doors, and the other characteristic issues that you have grown to love. I assure you, these "characteristics issues" will not be as appreciated by a perspective homebuyer — or their home inspector.

Just to be clear, a home inspector is almost always confused with an appraiser. A home inspector determines the condition of a structure, whereas an appraiser determines the value of a property. The inspector works for the client, and the appraiser works for the bank.

The home inspection is normally referred to as the "deal-killer". Obviously, you would want to mitigate anything that could possibly challenge the already delicate negotiation; especially considering the wide variance of experience within the cooperating real estate agents, not to mention their unspoken motivations.

Whoever orders it; a home inspection is a limited and non-invasive examination of the condition of a home. A home inspector who has the training, certifications and/or license to perform the inspection generally conducts the home inspection. The inspector is hired, conducts the inspection, and then prepares and delivers to their client a written report of their findings. The client then uses the findings to make informed decisions about either they're pending real estate purchase (if the client is the buyer), or the possibility of listing the home (if the client is a seller).

If the seller happens to be the client, then this inspection would be considered to be a "pre-inspection". The home inspector provides a snapshot understanding of the property condition but does not guarantee any future condition, efficiency, or life expectancy of any systems or components.

A further consideration is to have the basis needed to perform a return on investment analysis on larger ticket items that need to be addressed prior to listing your home. Please understand that you will not ever get a dollar for dollar return on your repairs. Think of it like this:

When you purchase a car, does the sales person tell you, "Yes, sir . . . this is a great purchase . . .", And then you realize that there is no windshield in the vehicle. Would you actually entertain a sales person asking you for a higher price if a windshield were installed with the purchase? No. So, then why would someone want to spend more for a home that has a new heat pump or A/C unit; or a new roof for that matter? You wouldn't and therefore, nor would a buyer; so don't get lulled in to this line of thinking. It is dangerous and irrational. If something needs to be repaired, than uncover it and fix it; or provide an allowance payable upon closing for that issue to be resolved so long as the appraisal allows that to pass.

What am I talking about as far as "inspection phase" and "negotiation phase"? During the initial offer, the buyer's agent will put a value (usually $500-$2500 depending) in an offer that defines the seller's responsibility for a repair cap. That repair cap will be the value (if you accept the offer) that you will have to come up with in order to correct any issues cited and prioritized by the buyer on a treatment/replacement/repair form. If agreeable, you (the seller) will have to correct these deficiencies prior to your agreed upon closing date. Instead, why not get a full understanding of all of the issues that will eventually come up any way and get them correct in your terms?

Going into a multi-thousand dollar negotiation, I know that I would much rather have a say in anything that would eventually be used against me. Getting your home pre-inspected prior to entering into a listing discussion effectively takes the wind out of the buyer's agent's billows. This cap value is one of the values that will be deducted from your seller net sheet. Just a thought, a home inspection costs $250. The repair cap that will be written into an offer presented to you will have a value of up to $2500. This is a no-brainer.

An inspector generally checks the roof, basement, heating system, water heater, air-conditioning system, structure, plumbing, electrical, and many other aspects of associated structures in order to identify improper building practices. A home inspection is not technical in nature nor implies that each item identified will be addressed. The home inspection is not the basis for a warranty or an obligation by the seller to correct anything.

If you remember in the introduction, there was mention of the "TRR", or the treatment, replacement, repair form. The buyer's agent generally fills out this form after the client has received the inspection report. This form is the basis for formal request from the buyer to the seller to correct any of the items identified during the inspection process.

I am sure that you can immediately see the advantage of getting a pre-inspection done prior to listing your home. Regardless of how you feel about your castle, that $250 is still incredibly less money that will be deducted from your net sheet. Identify the problems now and call your brother/uncle/babysitter's dad/etc., and get this stuff fixed.

The second part of this process is to get a pre-inspection and re-inspection. Ridicules or not, you need to identify what was wrong . . . proven that you have fixed it, and then provide a report. This will be the basis for which you can refuse a requested $2500 repair cap in a received offer. Make that inspection available as part of the seller's disclosure package. The more transparent you are, the better.

Chapter 9

Pre-paids, Buyer Closing Costs
and External Agencies

I have gone pretty far afield thus far in discussing the various things that will come up during the process, but the understanding of the concept of "pre-paids" is incredibly important; especially as a buyer.

Pre-paids will not go away. These are costs that either the buyer or the seller can pay. These are not funds that can be excused or set aside. In good form, the buyer should pay for his or her own pre-paids; but if they can't, there are ways to ask the seller to cover these costs.

What the heck are "pre-paids"? Pre-paids are payments that are made prior to payment being due or settlement has been conducted. Some common examples of pre-paids are mortgage interest, real estate taxes and homeowner's insurance.

Mortgage interest deals with the interest charged for a loan that is taken by the buyer and in this case, refers to the amount that accrues from the date of closing through the end of that calendar month. Pro-rated real estate taxes are another example of pre-paids. These taxes are the taxes that are normally assessed by the county and need to be paid into the buyer's escrow account prior to closing.

Some circumstances allow this to be handled differently, i.e., the use of a conventional loan for the financing. This amount will be paid out in increments of 12 along with your principle payment. This escrow management is normally taken care of by your lender. Also, there is your homeowner's (hazard) insurance that is also paid up to 1-year in advance and divvied up the same as the real estate taxes. These payments are all combined to form your monthly mortgage payment.

The other fees associated with settlement are below and are also generally required in order to make a deal safe and legal. Even if you were to sell your home as a For Sale by Owner (FiSBO), these are fees that will also not go away. Some of them can obviously be mitigated, but others cannot be avoided. Examples and a slight discussion of some of these fees might include the following:

Attorney Fees: Either party can pay Attorney Fees. These fees are either flat rates or retainers that pay for the preparation, review, and filing or recording (if necessary) of associated documents. Residential real estate deals generally use an attorney's opinion with determining the validity of title and abstract issues while commercial real estate is a bit more complex and costly.

Title Service: Title service can be paid by either the buyer or the seller and is directed by the contract. The Seller will likely pay most of this cost anyway because they will be required to bring their title up to date. This means that they pay someone to conduct a gap search on the existing and all prior title and then pay for the corresponding abstract to be updated. Further, the seller will usually purchase title insurance as an act of good faith to the buyer. Title insurance basically provides that if any lien comes against that title after closing, the carrier of that title will not be held responsible; the title agency that conducted the gap search and up date; however, will be.

That simply means that the title service company will pay whatever is required to "quiet" the title on behalf of the new titleholder. In some cases, an attorney may specialize in this; however, it is much less expensive for a title service company to do it. There is still an opportunity for the attorney opinion to double check the work.

Recording Fees: Either the buyer or the seller can pay recording Fees. These fees are charged by city, county or state for the action of entering an official record of the transference of rights to the property. This transference is generally referred to as the "recording of the deed".

Document Stamps: Doc stamps can be paid by either party depending on the jurisdiction that the transference of the rights of the property (or more simply, "the sale") took place; this is more commonly referred to as "excise tax" based upon the amount of the transaction. Local and/or State law requires this tax.

The survey fee is paid by either party and is done to simply confirm lot size and dimension, as well as to check for encroachments. This is a requirement by lenders and supports the appraisal. Fun fact, (in some States) if there is an encroachment that is not corrected in a specified period of time, then eventually, that encroachment becomes the property of the "encroaching" party. Again, you can see the necessity in making sure that you define and secure the actual property lines so that you may exercise your rights as you see fit.

Mortgage application Fees: These are fees specified by the lender to the seller within the GFE. I think of these fees as overhead that can be negotiated and reduced, depending on your ability to get your lender to maintain interest in doing business with them. These fees can be paid up front or as part of the settlement at the closing table.

I understand that everyone has got to make a living, and these fees go to paying the hourly pay of the mortgage loan processors, and later, the under-writers . . . as well as the light bill and is considered to be a cost associated with some service being provided . . . but, the amounts associated with this charge are purely arbitrary and as a buyer, and should try to be negotiate away. It is important to remember that there are several other lines of income deriving from a single transaction, so the mortgage lender loosing this one won't necessarily hurt anything. Further, most mortgage lenders are compensated (or upgraded) by their gross combined income (GCI) earnings for the company. This means that they get a raise based on their volume over a period of time, not over transaction fees taken. Sorry lenders, but don't worry. I will be talking about transaction fees derived from brokerages as well.

Points are a closing cost paid by the buyer to the lender. A "point" is a form is prepaid interest, which serves as a reduction to a quoted interest rate. Generally speaking, if someone qualifies for a loan, but at a higher interest rate then they really want to pay over the next 30-years, and they have the cash in hand; that buyer can "buy down" that interest rate. Depending on prevailing market conditions, one point usually equals one percent of the loan principal and occurs in increments of 0.125% (1/8th of a percent).

Points are fun, because if you have a savvy buyer's agent, then may be able to negotiate your "points" as part of the closing costs that may be being asked to get paid for by the seller. Think about it; how stupid is that? "I want to sell you my house so bad, I am going to somehow agree to purchase for you, the buyer with the crappy loan pre-qualification, your lower rate which will be in effect over the next 30-years. Seriously? Trust me, it happens.

The buyer usually pays the lender for appraisal fees. Depending on the area, banks will charge up to $450 for an appraisal. This fee is a requirement with anything that requires financing. This is normally specified as a condition that has to be met within the mortgage loan. The appraisal is basically a comparison analysis that verifies that the sales price is less than or equal to the fair market value of the same property. The appraisal serves as the basis for a loan to be given and secured by that same property.

Appraisals are carried out by licensed and trained individuals that are selected by some means as directed by that state. Many times, there is a pool where an appraisal request is submitted and then "picked up" by a random participating appraisal. This prohibits manipulation by the lender to use a specific appraiser for a specific appraisal.

It is also incredibly important to realize that the CMA (remember the beginning of the book; the "comparative market analysis"?) is based on the same techniques as the appraisal; however, the CMA is not being conducted by a trained or a licensed individual and is based on incomplete and un-updated data as gleaned by that real estate agent. Agents do not have the tools to conduct this sort of analysis to any structured or consistent degree.

A good example: Let's say that you have a beautiful 2-story, centerpiece to the established neighborhood and you have two competing listing agents come to you with their ideas of how they are going to get your home sold and what would be the right price point to position your home. One gives you a solid analysis of market conditions and a high/low estimate of where it "could" be placed, and leaves that decision up to you, with you having the final say-so as to where to price your home. You have the data to support your pricing decision.

Then, the next listing agent arrives and says, "The place around the corner is essentially the same as yours, but I like yours better. Did you know that a non-connected 2-car garage is worth $10k on an appraisal comp? We should probably add $10k to whatever the competition is asking just to make sure that you get everything that you deserve in price for your home". See where I am going with this? If someone comes to your doorstep touting "CMA", punch him or her in the mouth and slam the door.

If you go with them and that method, your home will sit at a price point that is not relevant to the current market; and will thus be rejected by that market, which as you know now is about as moveable as your house. Appraisals are important to lenders, but should not be used as a basis for pricing anything for these very reasons.

Another consideration is that an appraisal is simply a confirmation of fair market value. If a home sells for $215.9k, do you think that it is any huge coincidence that the appraisal comes back at $216k? Appraisals don't capture the motivated seller, the awful and ongoing divorce or separation, the change of job, etc. Like I said before, nothing happens until SOMETHING sells. Then you have a basis. Just be sure that you pay attention to the metrics that are being used to illustrate some point or another.

A home inspection can be paid as part of closing if an invoice is provided; however, these are generally paid upon completion of the home inspection. Inspectors are licensed and trained and generally do the same level of work.

It is important to remember that if you are the seller and you have paid for a pre-inspection, it is still the buyer's discretion to pay for their own inspection as part of the time period specification as determined by that State. The pre-inspection and the inspection are identical; the only difference being, who commissioned it.

If there is a pre-inspection associated with a listing, a buyer's agent may or may not counter with the idea that the seller purchased it; and therefore, should not be trusted. This is complete BS in that these are licensed individuals conducting the same level of work for the same price they would have charged you the buyer.

Other parts of the inspection process may be requirements by the lender, i.e., a pest or a termite inspection. Professionals in that field would carry these inspections out. This part of the inspection process also serves as an assurance that the property is capable of retaining the needed collateral value as specified by the mortgage lender.

Home warranties can be paid be either party. These are policies that help offer some modicum of assurance to the buyer that the major household systems and appliances will hold up for the first year of home ownership. These policies cover repair and replacement (generally with a specified cap) and also offer the holder of the policy an opportunity to pay a healthy co-pay for a participating local affiliate to come out and either flick a switch or do a major repair. If they show up, you pay them up to $75 for the contractual co-pay. Home warranties are regularly used as a marketing strategy, but if the home being purchased is a "re-do", then don't be surprised with the seller refuses to pay for the buyer's home warranty. Buyers regularly use home warranties as negotiation "throw-a-ways".

The final, and the largest of all of the closing costs are referred to as "Brokerage Commission". As I spelled out before, this is paid from the seller to the listing real estate brokerage in order to compensate that agency for their services. Those services are only as limited as are the imaginations of those that continually seek to provide padded package plans for the marketing, buyer lead generation and assistance in negotiations as needed in the listing and eventual sale of your home. Remember "IDX"?

These commissions are represented as percentages of the gross sales price and are established in the listing arrangement between the seller and the listing broker. The buyer side commission is also established within the listing agreement between the seller and the listing agent. This part of the commission agreement is paid to the buyer's agent brokerage upon close of the transaction.

Chapter 10

Transaction Fees

There are other lines of revenue that are admissible in some markets. Think about this example: You are driving in your neighborhood and you see your neighbor's kid on the side of the road with a shanty shack and the words "Lemonade—$0.25". You decide to stop and as you are paying for your cool, freshly squeezed beverage, made with the innocent hands of some kid; he stops you and says, "One second, sir. I don't know if you saw this written on the sign, but there is a transaction fee associated with this sale", "that will be an additional $0.50." You ask "why", and are given the explanation of something having to do with superb client treatment and an expert touch in the preparation of your cool, delicious drink. You laugh; you pay it, "whatever", right?

The listing side and the buying side of the transaction are both organized in a manner that legally allows either side to introduce any transaction fee that they see fit. It is a fee that is over and above the agreed commission and in some markets will be classified as part of the buyer's closing costs. Let me repeat that. You the seller will likely be asked to pay this innocuous fee on behalf of the buyer. Let me show you how.

Somewhere in the contract there will be a section that a buyer's agent can introduce specific inclusionary language. This area is designed to be able to capture the individual quirks that appear within every sale. But what do you do when you are presented with the following: "Seller to pay buyer closing costs to include pre-paids, allowables, non-allowables, and origination and transaction fees in an amount not to exceed $4500."

Before we get too far, the terms "allowables" and "non-allowables" have to do with government-backed loans, i.e., FHA and VA. Non-allowables include the underwriting fee, the loan processing fee, the mortgage broker fee, any administration fees, tax service fee, wire fee and any associated escrow fees . . . allowables are everything else.

These government mortgage loan programs decided early on that they wanted to protect the purchaser (as they were generally associated with some sort of government work) and just say that they would not authorize the loan if the borrower paid any of those fees.

Look again at the example arbitrary $4500 example. You, the seller, were just given a hard cap of $4500 that you will be deducting from your seller's net sheet that your listing agent has no doubt prepared for you. Chances are, you have already accounted for this cost as a worst-case scenario and if the difference is above your net goal, then you will likely accept the offer.

Do you see how you the seller were just taken for an additional transaction fee, however small? By the way, do you remember your listing agreement? Did that happen to have a transaction fee associated with it as well? I'll bet it did.

You want to know something else? That hard working buyer's agent was probably told, "If you don't get that transaction fee, that transaction fee amount will be deducted from your commission split at the close of this sale." Based on that, it is fair to assume that the buyer side transaction fee does not even go to the agent; it is simply another line of revenue that gets back to the brokerage. But how is this legal?

RESPA stands for the "Real Estate Settlement Procedures Act", and can be referenced: http://www.federalreserve.gov/boarddocs/supmanual/cch/respa.pdf

Section 8 of RESPA prohibits anyone from giving or accepting a fee, kickback or anything of value in exchange for referrals of settlement service business involving federally related mortgage loans. To go further, RESPA also prohibits fee splitting and **receiving unearned fees for services <u>not actually performed</u>**. Violations of this act are subject to criminal and civil penalties.

Prohibition Against Kickbacks and Unearned Fees (§3500.14)

> "Any person who gives or receives a fee or a thing of value (payments, commissions, fees, gifts or special privileges) for the referral of settlement business is in violation of section 8 of RESPA. Payments in excess of the reasonable value of goods provided or services rendered are consideredw unearned fees. Appendix B of Regulation X provides guidance on the meaning and coverage of the prohibition against kickbacks and unearned fees."

Interestingly, Appendix B of Regulation X has to do specifically with mortgage brokers, not real estate brokers. What this means is simply, the margin surrounding the term "broker" allows broad application—in my opinion.

The brokerages that do this are imposing a self-determined fee independent of any specific action which would have otherwise been done by realtor, broker or broker's staff, to get a transaction complete and through to closing. One method of staying safe, at least from the perspective of the real estate professional is the action of disclosing a transaction fee up front, and getting you to sign something in agreement to those terms.

RESPA allows for fees of this nature; however, those fees must be communicated and completed. Again, the flip side is that all of those "communicated ideas" are things that are going to be completed anyway in order to get your deal done. Generally, if you (the buyer) have a reservation about this minor transaction fee, then the agent will likely say something to the effect of: "don't worry about it, this is a transaction fee and will be paid as part of your closing. If you remember, we are asking the seller to pay for your closing costs." Of course, you agree.

Due to the language of RESPA, you, the seller, are likely being opened up to a prodigious and predatory billing for services that should already be taking place as a matter of course in getting the deal done; which is in the buyer brokerage's financial interest. I know, it's less than $500, but take that times 84 transactions a year, times 4 agents . . . and then double that if you consider the listing side as well: $336,000, conservatively.

This little trick; however legally unchallenged or manipulated, results in an incredibly powerful influx of income to the industry in general. It is unchecked, and as long as you agree to it when you sign the disclosure section of the any State's buyer brokerage agreement; there is nothing more that you can do about it; but hey . . . its not your problem anyway, because you have already asked the seller to pay your closing costs "to include pre-paids, allowable, non-allowables, origination and transaction fees in an amount not to exceed".

Remember how I mentioned that the buyer's interests would be leveraged against the previously existing agreement between the listing agent and the seller?

If the buyer agent wants to not get that transaction fee deducted from their justified and agreed upon earnings (if that is the case), that buyer's agent will say something to the following: "we will negotiate that the seller take care of this cost on your behalf". You agree and don't care, because in your mind, you are not paying it. The seller doesn't care either, because they a) weren't told about it until the HUD-1 settlement statement was received for review, or b) they were given a "cap" to simply deduct from their net which gave them the ability to make a decision as to whether or not to take the deal.

Based on these legally binding constraints, and the increased margins created by those very constraints, as well as the allowed (and encouraged) flexibilities within the law; wouldn't you say that it is a particularly dangerous undertaking, financially speaking, to be a seller in any market?

I am mentioning RESPA only to bring your attention to it. Further, it isn't my intention to try and paint every agent and every broker to be dishonest, which just isn't the case. The better agency will take a higher path and will likely not participate in any such practice out of principle unless they have a proven repeatable system that can be disclosed up-front.

Right now, I am simply trying to give you the tools and vocabulary that you should have at your disposal prior to talking to any agent. Hopefully what you have read thus far will help you realize the difference between a "pro" who is interested in getting you what you want and clearly understands that he or she will not get rich from any one deal.

I have included a standard buyer broker service agreement below for you to see just how this works. This is important, because if you sign this as a buyer that means that you are only going to be doing business with that agent. You will eventually sign something like this, but only right before an offer needs to be submitted on your behalf.

Without this in place, the agent cannot act even as a transaction broker representative and deliver offers or accept counter offers for you.

Careful though, if you agree and sign this, then you will be held responsible to pay whatever the terms you agreed to within the compensation portion of this agreement, as well as what ever terms you came to with what ever agent you decided to go to halfway through the process.

These agreements are designed to identify in a clear way who's client is who's in order to eliminate inappropriate behavior as well as to limit the ethically questionable practice of stealing someone's lead. In a way, this form protects the agent and their brokerage's time and resources from being taken advantage of by a buyer. Don't think this is form is used to trap you; it is used to identify compensation and relationship between two parties. Here is an example of a standard buyer broker agreement:

BUYER BROKER SERVICE AGREEMENT

1. Purpose of Brokerage. Buyer desires to purchase, lease, option or exchange (collectively "Purchase") real estate through the services and resources of the Broker. Broker's services may include, but not be limited to, consulting with Buyer regarding particular properties and the availability of financing; formulating acquisition and purchase agreements and receiving delivery of any offers made by Buyer and accepted by Seller. Note: If this form is used as part of a lease or rental transaction, the term "Seller" shall be deemed to mean "Landlord", and the term "Buyer" shall be deemed to mean "Tenant".

2. Buyer's Acknowledgement. a. Buyer represents that Buyer has not signed a written brokerage agreement currently in force with another Broker. b. Buyer is not relying on Broker to determine the suitability of any desired property for the Buyer's purposes or regarding the environmental or other condition of the desired property. Broker shall not be obligated to discover latent defects in the desired property or to advise on matters outside of the scope of his/her real estate license. Broker does not make any representation or warranty with respect to the advisability of, or the legal effect of, any transaction contemplated by Buyer. Broker shall cooperate fully with any legal counsel of Buyer's choice. Broker is not an expert in matters relating to law, tax, financing, surveying, structural condition, hazardous materials, engineering or other highly specialized areas. Broker hereby advises Buyer to seek professional advice relating to these matters.

3. Duration of Agreement. This Agreement is entered into this _____ day of _____, 20__. This Agreement shall expire on the _____ day of _____, 20__. This Agreement may be canceled only by the mutual consent of the parties in writing. Buyer agrees during the term of this Agreement, any and all inquiries and/or negotiations relating to the acquisition by the Buyer of any desired property shall be through the undersigned Broker.

4. Compensation of Broker. Broker shall be compensated in the following manner (check one):

    ___ a. By acceptance of the amount of compensation offered by a Listing Broker or the Seller
    ___ b. Buyer shall pay the Broker, at closing, an amount equal to $_____ or ____% of the gross selling price. Buyer shall receive a credit towards the payment of Broker's compensation

in an amount equal to any payment made to the Broker by any other Broker or the Seller.

__ c. Buyer shall pay Broker a retainer fee of $_____ due and payable upon execution of this Agreement, which amount shall be applied towards Broker's compensation upon closing on a transaction in which Buyer acquires Property. In all other circumstances, the payment shall be considered as a non-refundable retainer fee earned by the Broker.

__ d. Other: _____

> **Interjection: (In _"4.d. Other"_ you may or may not see language to the affect: "Jack and Jill Real Estate Brokerage Superstars transaction fee: $595".)**

Unless otherwise specified above, the compensation is due and payable upon Closing. The compensation shall apply to any purchase agreements executed during the term of this Agreement, or during any extension of this Agreement. The compensation will also apply to purchase agreements executed within _____ days (or 90 days if left blank) after the expiration or other termination of this Agreement, if the property acquired was presented to Buyer through the services of Broker. If Seller fails to close with no fault on the part of Buyer, the compensation shall be waived. If the transaction does not close due to a breach of the Contract of Sale by the Buyer, the compensation shall NOT be waived and shall become immediately due and payable.

5. Cost of Services or Products Obtained from Outside Sources. Broker will not obtain or order products or services from outside sources (e.g., surveys, soil tests, title reports, inspections) without the prior consent of Buyer, unless provided by the Contract of Sale, Lease, Option or Exchange of Real Estate. Buyer agrees to

pay all costs for products or services so obtained. Broker shall not be obligated to advance funds for Buyer.

6. Brokerage Relationship. Buyer and Broker confirm that prior to signing this Agreement, both Buyer and Broker understand, agree and confirm the Brokerage Relationship selected below:

___ Transaction Broker Disclosure

OR

___ Single-Party Broker Disclosure

7. Other Buyers. Buyer understands that other buyers may consider, make offers, or purchase through Broker the same or similar properties as Buyer is seeking to acquire. Within the same company, the Broker and their associated licensees including the licensee assisting you, often provide brokerage services to more than one buyer at the same time.

8. Equal Opportunity. Properties shall be shown and be made available to Buyer without regard to age, race, color, religion, sex, handicap, familial status, national origin or as may be provided by local, state or federal laws or regulations.

9. Additional Provisions.

_____

10. Counterparts. If more than one person is named as Buyer herein, separate each Buyer may execute conforming Agreements individually, and when so executed, such copies taken together shall be deemed to be a full and complete agreement between the Parties.

11. Copy of Agreement. Buyer acknowledges receipt of

    (a) a copy of this Agreement,

    (b) a copy of the Disclosure regarding Real Estate Brokerage Relationship and

    (c) that a Oklahoma Uniform Contract Information Pamphlet has been made available to Buyer. Executed by Buyer this _____ day of _____, 20_____.

As I indicated in my "interjection", Paragraph 4.d. "Other" is generally where someone would write in a disclosure of a transaction fee that I mentioned in reference to the RESPA dialogue from before. If you remember the language from the RESPA stuff I cited before, you should remember the terms "unearned fees".

If you agree to pay this fee, or if you agree to sign up for this fee and then have someone else pay it on your behalf as it will be grouped under the umbrella of "buyer closing costs", just be sure that your real estate professional can succinctly describe and demonstrate exactly what that transaction fee of $595 (in this example) is buying. If they do so to your satisfaction, they are safe; otherwise, demand it be left off of the transaction.

A bad example of a justification for this fee might be, "this transaction fee goes to the overhead associated with our hourly paid processors within the agency". This is something that would be being paid for already as something that needs to be done in order that the sale passes; i.e., paying staff salary. What a good example might look like would be something to the effect of some buyer superstar program that has an itemized breakdown of how that agency is going to go above and beyond for you. Don't worry, that will be generally written as well.

Just remember, that by "buying" into this income stream, you are allowing yourself to be used as leverage against the seller in order to maximize earnings to the brokerages involved without any benefit whatsoever being gained by you.

Chapter 11

Buyer Agent Perspective

Now that you have somewhat of a basis for all of this, I want to share with you what we see from the other side of the table. It isn't bad, but by paying attention to a few of these cues, you will be able to more effectively assert your position when you are facing your listing agent.

Before we get into this lesson in common sense, I want you to realize the power of accountability. Everyone wants to be held accountable. To be held accountable in a small thing means that you have some other person stopping what they are doing to simply ask how you are doing on "such-and-such". You immediately feel connected to an idea and want to do well because you have another rational person accepting your good effort and giving you some sort of praise. You don't want to fail in that small thing, because you don't want to make an excuse or let down your newfound accountability partner. Isn't it crazy to think just how many people seek someone just to keep them accountable to them selves and their own personal goals?

Ok, where am I going with this, you ask? It is simple, when you come in and sit down in front of me, you have a pretty good idea of at least what you need, not so much of what you want. This goes for both client types (buyers and sellers). I will sit and listen to you; but when ever you start going off on a tangent, I will subtly re-direct you back to the reason you are in front of me taking my time.

By listening, not talking, not interrupting, I am determining your personality type. I am also allowing you to fill the air with your thoughts. Further, by listening, not talking, not interrupting, I am taking note of all of the different ways that I will be matching your tone as well as holding you accountable for either your understanding or your lack of understanding of not only the process, but of which direction I want you to go. Listen for me to use little redirect cues that sound like: "I appreciate your position, and I am sure that you would agree that . . . ."

Essentially, I am going to make you feel accountable for your goals either succeeding or failing. I am going to do this by using language and concept ideas that you haven't heard of before, and by doing that; I am going to be construed by you as a collaborative expert in the subject matter at hand; a resource. Then, I am going to give you a chance to buy into the personal accountability that you are going to have to impose on yourself in order for you to get what you just said you wanted. I am going to advise you; I am not going to push anything, and you will be making your own decisions . . . or will you be?

Interestingly, you can apply this same principle to your situation, except that you will be controlling the pace. This is possible only if you do your homework up front.

As a buyer, please consider that there isn't really anything worth having that you have to finance yourself to death over. You know your budget; make a plan a year out as to what kind of payment you will be able to manage.

Think of that amount as a total increment that includes principle, interest, taxes and insurance (and in some cases, mortgage insurance). Based on that, it is pretty simple to do an Internet search for the prevailing rates of different loan types and term length. Then, just get a simple amortization calculator, which will give you a principle balance breakdown. Run your calculations for a random house price number and get your monthly principle payment at the interest rate you just found on the Internet. Write that down, that is part one and two (or your principle and interest parts).

Part 3 and 4 are pretty similar. For your taxes, you can look them up in your area or just estimate 0.75% of your imaginary purchase price. Figure that number out and then divide that by 12 (Taxes are paid backwards). Write that number down. Do the same thing for your hazard insurance (Insurance is paid forward), but at a rate of around 2.1%. Figure that number out and divide that by 12. Write that number down.

Add all those numbers up and voila, there is your total estimated monthly payment for your new imaginary house. As you begin to play with the numbers you will see a few different relationships pop up. You will see that the only things that drastically affect your mortgage payment will be your taxes or your insurance. Keep that in mind because when you receive that phone call that says something to the affect of "rates have never been lower", you will know that this is only half of the story. Good rates are important, but so is maintain your credit history so that you can get a good insurance quote.

The other relationship that you should be able to put together is the minor variance in principle monthly payments when comparing large differences in purchase price. An example would be the principle and interest difference between $100,000 at 4% over 30 years and $110,000 at 4% over 30 years. Any ideas? The answer is $525.16 - 477.42$ equaling $47.74. Not much, huh? Be careful with this idea, because it will be used to upsell you. The point is that you need to have a good idea of what exactly you can afford and then start preparing for it.

Again, here is a brief breakdown (as a buyer) of what up-front costs you should prepare yourself for prior to visiting with a real estate agent:

- 5% of the estimated purchase price for a down payment.
- 2.5% of the estimated purchase price for your closing costs
- 0.5-1% of the estimated purchase price for your earnest money payment that will accompany your offer
- Around $250 for a home inspection
- Around $450 for an appraisal

I used a value of 5% for your down payment because it is within the realm of an ideal type of loan, which is called a Conventional loan (there are programs out there that get you to the remaining 20% down). These give the buyer the most flexibility, and get you into your principle more quickly. In other words, people who do not need government assistance to subsidize a down payment use these loans. Talk to a lender about putting 5% instead of 20% down. They will help you though the process. I also used 5%, because it is bigger than 3.5%, which is the down payment amount generally needed for an FHA loan.

If you had all of these items in order prior to seeing a real estate agent, you would be considered "golden". Having planned for these values doesn't necessarily mean that you will use them; it just means that you have a contingency in the event the seller isn't in a position to give you all that you want, i.e., your closing costs, etc. By doing this, I am sure that you can see the huge advantage you will have during the negotiation phase of your home buying effort.

Here is an example of how being prepared like this would work to your advantage:

You find a home that is priced at $275,000. It is a bit older, and your agent tells you that there may be some lender-required repairs (from the appraisal) that may come up. Hopefully, he or she advises you that Conventional loans are much less picky within their guidelines, thus allowing your mortgage lender's underwriters to mitigate risk more easily. Remember, it isn't only you that has to qualify for your loan, so does the house that you have selected. You are also told that a conventional loan will hold a higher weight in the seller's eyes if a multiple offer situation arises (for the same reasons).

Make your earnest money "payment" a high amount as well. This is interesting because a higher amount used for earnest money makes it seem as if you have a stronger offer. This isn't really the case at all as lenders will generally get that earnest money back for you at closing. The seller will not likely see that money; but it gives a good impression.

You know that you already have your closing costs in savings, and you also know that the listing price will very well have the closing costs built in. Deduct your estimate of closing costs off the asking price right off the bat and then still ask for your closing to be covered by the seller.

From the prior discussion, you also know that a listing agency has an agreement in place with this seller. It basically states that they will be receiving a compensation of X% of purchase price. This is a value that they agreed to pay.

It is not your concern if the home has to sell in order that the listing agency gets paid, it should be your concern however, that you are financing that listing commission on behalf of the seller. So deduct another 3% (estimated) off the purchase price.

$275,000 – $6875 closing – $8250 listing commissions = Offer of $259,875 and still ask for your closing to be paid by the seller.

This looks good, but is arbitrary. The listing commissions will be paid regardless of the purchase price, so in this example (if accepted), a listing commission of $7796 will still be paid from proceeds gained by the seller. The point is, don't get wrapped up in the buyer side commission piece as a buyer. Just make an offer that you know that you can afford to maintain. Very likely, that example above will be countered with purchase price to be $267,437.50 and seller pays buyer closing. In other words, the seller split the difference in price-point and gave you what you asked for.

Chapter 12

Chasing that last 1%

Well, that was a mouthful. I just gave you a lot of ideas that you really ought to understand in order to just have a conversation about selling your home. Do you remember us talking about the "sale assist" several chapters back? At the end of that chapter, I asked you if you wanted to know how to get after that last percent of your equity.

Listing with an agency is really the easy way out; and for some, it is the right answer. I am not talking about those minor few situations. My goal is to help you to understand what you can do to mitigate all unnecessary financial loss when selling your home.

I am not advocating the non-use of real estate professionals; nor am I advocating the dangerous path taken through the For Sale By Owner, or "FiSBO" as a seller. What I am going to tell you now is how you can position yourself to leverage a buyer's agent to your advantage as a home seller, and escape paying out a 3-4% listing commission.

Please understand that effective listing agencies will hold some form of the following ideas as their core principles: Only engage in activities that are lowest cost, have the highest ROI and are the easiest things to execute. Those are the three things that an effective business model is generally based on.

In order to protect yourself against being taken advantage of when dealing with highly organized listing agencies, consider these the following as necessary steps to take in preparation for selling your home:

- Get a pre-inspection, fix everything and get a re-inspection
- Purchase a home warranty that you can transfer to a buyer
- Rent a storage unit and de-clutter your home
- Stage your home
- Clean up curb appeal, get 2nd opinion

After you have done all this, find out what your principle balance for your payoff (if necessary) and then determine your "walk away from the deal number". Your sales price will have to include a 3% buyer's agent commission plus warranty (roughly $550) plus roughly 1.5% of total sales price for buyer's closing costs that you will concede in negotiations if necessary.

After you have all this done, call a random agent or agency and just ask them to tell you what the average sales price is for your area over the last two years. It will take approximately two whole minutes for them to pull and provide you that information. Call around if the first agency won't play.

Once you have that number, deduct 5% from that two-year average. That number is the highest number you should consider, and don't forget that this number includes all those values from above.

Here is the thinking: Homes that sell within the first 30-45 days are priced at 5-10% below market condition average, period. Travertine is nice, but a trailer in a trailer park with a travertine-laden bathroom is still a trailer. Don't forget that! After all of this prep work, purchase a "For Sale By Owner" sign, and stick it in your yard.

Here is what will happen next: every real estate agency in your market will have someone call you at the number you provided on the FiSBO sign. They will go through a long line of crap with you in order to set up an appointment and "offer" their help in getting your home sold. You agree to the appointment, but know in the back of your mind that you will only be offering a 3% commission to anyone who sells the home. The point is you want to get into the listing appointment and let them deliver their pitch. You want to make them commit to a number.

Because you have already done your homework, you are pretty much just listening for them to give you a number that is greater than the 5%-below-market-average-number that you have already determined. Once you hear that number, stand up and thank them and leave.

I know what you are thinking . . . "But what about all that other stuff", right? Here's the deal. That buyer agent, when one finally presents themselves, doesn't care where their 3% comes from, because that 3% is all they are used to getting . . . remember, that 3% to them isn't actually 3%, it is a split between them and the broker they work for; which that brokerage would be getting if they were involved in a co-brokerage transaction anyway.

From the brokerage's perspective, doing this deal means nothing different than if they were doing a regular deal. The buyer's agent that brought you that offer will be the only one that realizes the additional pain.

That agent will try to get you to sign a listing agreement and do a "sold when listed" type of thing. No worries, just say "no". This is commonly offered, and when you agree, the buyer they mentioned fails to materialize; and now you are in a listing agreement.

The agent will simply give you a compensation agreement that should state something to the affect of: "If brokerage 'such and such' produces a ready, willing and able buyer, and closes on the sale of my home, I will pay that brokerage 3% gross sales price upon close."

You might even offer a small bonus with an approved offer in a specific period of time. Either way, some agent will eventually bring you an offer, which you will agree to or not. If you agree, then that agent will be responsible for getting that deal worked through because it is in their interest to get paid. Further, all of the other issues that are kicked back and forth between the listing agent (or their representative) and the seller have to do with repairs.

These are the same repairs that you have already uncovered during your inspection and fixed . . . so there won't be any. Further, you are offering a warranty for your major appliances and also conceding some of the buyer's closing costs.

After the buyer's inspection period has ended and the appraisal has come back good, then order your abstract and direct that it go to whichever closing company that buyer's agent wants to use. It doesn't matter who, because now you are relying on that buyer agent's established professional network to get the gap search, attorney opinion and warranty deed worked up. The rest really falls onto the buyer getting their financing through underwriting.

The title company acts as a 3rd party broker and doesn't allow any thing to pass until all elements of the contract have been executed or made good.

So, here is an example: Lets say the average price sold in your area over the last few years has been $175k. That means that if you want to sell your home fast, you want to offer it for not much more than $166,250.

Out of that $166,250 you need to deduct 1.5% or $2493.75 for buyer closing concession, 3% or $4987.50 for the buyer's agent that you just tricked into doing all of your dirty work and then an additional $550 for a year's worth of a home-warranty that you are also going to get for the buyer.

When you do this, it leaves you a net value of: $158,218.75. This is 4.8% of your gross sales price versus the 12% that you would have been forced to swallow had you just gone to a listing agent. 12% equals $19,950, 4.8% equals $8031.25. That is a difference of $11,918.75. Could you use an additional $11,918.75?

Is there anything else to say?

Chapter 13

Responsibility

The system is unfortunately broken and will be forever stacked against the seller. This is not an idealistic attempt to change any system; instead, it is meant to serve as an aid to help you to understand, as well as to embrace, the existing system and use its structure to your advantage.

The people involved in real estate are all good people and when given the opportunity to fight for your interests, they, as individuals, will fight for your interests to the best of their ability. Use their willingness to your advantage. They are very likely just barely hanging on and have a difficult time telling you "no". Just be smart about how you proceed; and you will do very well.

Consider what the buyer agent sees when they are qualifying prospective leads. You can do the same with buyer agents as a seller. There are many of them and one of you.

"Real Estate" in-and-of-itself will never offer the binding features that are present in securities or other monetarily based markets. The interesting part about this is that the real estate industry has a parasitic dependence on parallel industries' regulations. It is within these other industries regulations that allow for basic transactions to close in an appropriate manner. Therefore, when you are considering the throughput of the offer/contract process, it is easy to see why the concept of "sausage making" comes to mind. The process is not so nearly refined as it should be; yet, thousands of home sales close every day.

Regardless of the best efforts of any given real estate agent (I am thinking of the pen scrawled offers obviously written on the hood of a car and jammed in my office drop slot), rest assured that there are regulated systems in place that will make the deal legal and appropriate. These are the systems that you will depend upon to get your deals done, not the agent.

Just remember that the lack of experience within a common agent involved in your transaction is relative, and there will always be several other hands helping the transaction to move along; with our without your input. It is in everyone's best interest to close . . . they want to get paid.

Chapter 14

Why

Believe it or not, I can be a compassionate person. When I am faced with someone who's life can be significantly improved by the simple act of me taking a moment and just sharing some experiences and perspectives; I will try to help. In a given day, I have conversations with up to 40 clients or potential clients. I listen to their frustration and their experiences; and instead of empathizing or making excuses for some other agent's failure, I will ask you what they want. Before I ask that, I will ALWAYS ask "why". "Why" transcends all areas of "want".

What I do has nothing to do with sales. Even though I technically "sell" houses, I am doing nothing more than being an advisor. True, I do listen and keep you accountable for the priorities that you have made very clear to me (over and over usually); but at the end, I am able to lead you to exactly what you have already decided is perfect. Along the way, I will have also shared with you all of the appropriate ways to approach the system.

If there are any geeks reading this, think of how "object-oriented programs" act in simple computer gaming programing. The approach is quite simple and sounds something to the effect of "If X then Y". I am working to prepare your way of thinking to react in this manner. I am training you to recognize meaningful factors within any given situation that serve as indicators of how you should proceed.

If I have effectively listened to you, that means that before you walk into a home that you are considering for purchase, you are already thinking of all of the leverage points—not because of the condition of the house—but because of how the house is positioned within the market. You start thinking in terms of "if/then" and "cooperation", and in the process, you become very savvy. All of your anxiety goes away because you are in charge.

I want buyers and sellers to be informed. I want you to be informed because if that happens, erroneous charges and fees and inflated pricing will reduce. The greater (and obvious) effect will be a faster moving housing market. That "faster paced market" will then positively affect the economy. Demand will increase, thus slightly increasing (but quickly stabilizing) interest rates for lenders. Conversely, people who should not be buying houses in the first place will not be able to until they get their financial lives in order, thus reducing the shadow market made up by bank owned properties (Real Estate Owned, or "REO").

There will also be an impact on government involvement and manipulation of the housing market at large because under this model, government backed loans (VA, FHA) will be used less and less due to a heightened competition within the housing market.

This is all very exciting, but I know that this all will never pass. You can't really affect things from the grass-roots level unless all involved embrace these principles. The de-regulated activities of real estate professionals; who are just trying to survive within the system, actually dis-allows these ideas to work in a meaningful way. That very fact; however, demands that you use this information—simply because no one else is thinking this way.

The reality is that these ideas are bad for business (from a listing brokerage's perspective) and therefore, will never catch on. Despite the happy thoughts of a simple and systematic defense of another inflation burst within real estate, people will generally take the path of least resistance—especially when it comes to making money (i.e., high-margin business models).

This path is the margin for opening the doors that I referred to at the outset. You are simply leveraging accepted truths and interests to your advantage . . . and if done correctly, the payoff will be worth it. Your actions will be supported by the persistence of the systems already in place.

All of that said; consider the remarkable increase in return (that wasn't lost to systematic events) for the flip investor or the home-seller. Consider the reduced asking prices that would be experienced by the homebuyer. Is it worth your time and your money to simply ask the question? Well, now you know what questions to ask.

I look forward to your success through the application of these basic principles. Neither Agents nor Brokers will appreciate your knowledge of this material, but that doesn't really matter. Be smart. Let me help you through the process.

Appendix 1

Residential Contract of Sale of Real Estate (Example)

*This is a legally binding Contract if not understood seek advice from an attorney

CONTRACT DOCUMENTS. The Contract is defined as this document with the following attachment(s):

(check as applicable)

___ Conventional Loan   ___ Single Family Mandatory HOA
___ FHA Loan   ___ Condominium Association
___ VA Loan   ___ Townhouse Association
___ Assumption   ___ Supplement
___ Seller Financing   ___ Sale of Buyer's Property—Presently U/C
       ___ Sale of Buyer's Property—Not Under Contract

PARTIES. THE CONTRACT is entered into between:

_____

"Seller"

AND

_____

"Buyer"

The Parties' signatures at the end of the Contract, which includes any attachments or documents incorporated by reference, with delivery to their respective Brokers, if applicable, will create a valid and binding Contract, which sets forth their complete understanding of the terms of the Contract. This agreement shall be binding upon and inure to the benefit of the parties hereto and their respective heirs, successors and permitted assigns. The Contract shall be executed by original signatures of the parties or by signatures as reflected on separate identical Contract counterparts (carbon, photo or fax copies). The parties agree that as to all aspects of this transaction involving documents an electronic signature shall have the same force and effect as an original signature pursuant to the provisions of the Uniform Electronic Transactions Act, 12A, All prior verbal or written negotiations, representations and agreements are superseded by the Contract, which may only be modified or assigned by a further written agreement of Buyer and Seller. Seller agrees to sell and convey by General Warranty Deed, and Buyer agrees to accept such deed and buy the Property described herein, on the following terms and conditions:

The Property shall consist of the following described real estate located in _____ County, STATE.

1. LEGAL DESCRIPTION.

_____

Property Address City Zip

_____

Together with all fixtures and improvements, and all appurtenances, subject to existing zoning ordinances plat or deed restrictions, utility easements serving the Property, including all mineral rights owned by Seller, which may be subject to lease, unless expressly reserved by Seller in the Contract and excluding mineral rights previously reserved or conveyed of record (collectively referred to as "the Property".)

2. PURCHASE PRICE, EARNEST MONEY AND SOURCE OF FUNDS. This is a CASH TRANSACTION unless a Financing Supplement is attached. The Purchase Price is $_____ payable by Buyer as follows: Buyer has paid $_____ as Earnest Money on execution of the Contract, and Buyer shall pay the balance of the purchase price and Buyer's Closing costs at Closing. Upon execution of the Contract, the Earnest Money shall be deposited in the trust account of _____ _____or if left blank, the Listing Broker's trust account, as part payment of the purchase price and/or closing costs. No interest shall be accrued.

3. CLOSING, FUNDING AND POSSESSION. The Closing process includes execution of documents, delivery of deed and receipt of funds by Seller and shall be completed on or before _____, ("Closing Date") or not later than _____ days (five [5] days if left blank) thereafter caused by a delay of the Closing process, or such later date as may be necessary in the Title Evidence Paragraph of the Contract. Possession shall be transferred upon conclusion of closing process unless otherwise provided below:

_____.

In addition to costs and expenses otherwise required to be paid in accordance with terms of the Contract, Buyer shall pay Buyer's Closing fee, Buyer's recording fees, and all other expenses required from Buyer. Seller shall pay documentary stamps required, Seller's Closing fee, Seller's recording fees, if any, and all other expenses required from Seller. Funds required from Buyer and Seller at Closing shall be either cash, cashier's check or wire transfer. This form was created by the Oklahoma Real Estate Contract Form Committee and approved by the Oklahoma Real Estate Commission.

4. ACCESSORIES, EQUIPMENT AND SYSTEMS. The following items, if existing on the Property, unless otherwise excluded, shall remain with the Property at no additional cost to Buyer:

- Attic and ceiling fan(s)
- Bathroom mirror(s)
- Other mirrors, if attached
- Central vacuum & attachments
- Floor coverings, if attached
- Key(s) to the property
- Built-in and under cabinet/counter appliance(s)
- Free-standing slide-in/drop-in kitchen stove
- Built-in sound system(s)/speaker(s)
- Lighting & light fixtures
- Fire, smoke and security system(s), if owned
- Shelving, if attached
- Fireplace inserts, logs, grates, doors and screens
- Free standing heating unit(s)
- Humidifier(s), if attached
- Water conditioning systems, if owned
- Window treatments & coverings, interior & exterior
- Storm windows, screens & storm doors
- Garage door opener(s) & remote transmitting unit(s)

- Fences (includes sub-surface electric & components)
- Mailboxes/Flag poles
- Outside cooking unit(s), if attached
- Propane tank(s) if owned
- TV antennas/satellite dish system(s) and control(s), if owned
- Sprinkler systems & control(s)
- Swimming Pool/Spa equipment/accessories
- Attached recreational equipment
- Exterior landscaping and lighting
- Entry gate control(s)
- Water meter, sewer/trash membership, if owned
- All remote controls, if applicable
- Transferable Service Agreements and Product Warranties

A. Additional Inclusions. The following items shall also remain with the Property at no additional cost to Buyer:

_____.

B. Exclusions. The following items shall not remain with the Property:

_____.

5. TIME PERIODS SPECIFIED IN CONTRACT. Time periods for Investigations, Inspections and reviews and Financing Supplement shall commence on _____ (Time Reference date), regardless of the date the Contract is signed by Buyer and Seller. The day after the Time reference Date shall be counted as day one (1). If left blank, the Time reference Date shall be the third day after the last date of signatures of the parties.

6. RESIDENTIAL PROPERTY CONDITION DISCLOSURE. No representations by Seller regarding the condition of Property or environmental hazards are expressed or implied, other than as specified in a residential Property Condition Disclosure Statement ("Disclosure Statement") or a Property Condition Disclaimer Statement ("Disclaimer Statement"), if applicable. A real estate licensee has no duty to Seller or Buyer to conduct an independent inspection of the Property and has no duty to independently verify accuracy or completeness of any statement made by Seller in the Disclosure Statement and any amendment or the Disclaimer Statement.

7. INVESTIGATIONS, INSPECTIONS and REVIEWS.

   A. Buyer shall have _____ days (10 days if left blank) after the Time reference Date to complete any investigations, inspections, and reviews. Seller shall have water, gas and electricity turned on and serving the Property for Buyer's inspections, and through the date of possession or Closing, whichever occurs first. If required by ordinance, Seller, or Seller's Broker, if applicable, shall deliver to Buyer, in care of Buyer's Broker, if applicable, within five (5) days after the Time reference Date any written notices affecting the Property.

   B. Buyer, together with persons deemed qualified by Buyer and at Buyer's expense, shall have the right to enter upon the Property to conduct any and all investigations, inspections, and reviews of the Property. Buyer's right to enter upon the Property shall extend to licensed Home Inspectors and licensed architects for purposes of performing a home inspection. Buyer's right to enter upon the Property shall also extend to registered professional engineers, professional craftsman and/

or other individuals retained by Buyer to perform a limited or specialized investigation, inspection or review of the Property pursuant to a license or registration from the appropriate State licensing board, commission or department. Finally, Buyer's right to enter upon the Property shall extend to any other person representing Buyer to conduct an investigation, inspection and/or review which is lawful but otherwise unregulated or unlicensed under the Law. Buyer's investigations, inspections, and reviews may include, but not be limited to, the following:

1) Disclosure Statement or disclaimer Statement unless exempt
2) Flood, Storm Run off Water, Storm Sewer Backup or Water History
3) Psychologically Impacted Property and Megan's Law
4) Hazard Insurance (Property insurability)
5) Environmental Risks, including, but not limited to soil, air, water, hydrocarbon, chemical, carbon, asbestos, mold, radon gas, lead-based paint
6) Roof, structural members, roof decking, coverings and related components
7) Home Inspection
8) Structural Inspection
9) Fixtures, Equipment and Systems Inspection. All fixtures, equipment and systems relating to plumbing (including sewer/septic system and water supply), heating, cooling, electrical, built-in appliances, swimming pool, spa, sprinkler systems, and security systems.
10) Termites and other Wood destroying Insects Inspection
11) Use of Property. Property use restrictions, building restrictions, easements, restrictive covenants, zoning ordinances and regulations, mandatory Homeowner Associations and dues

12) Square Footage. Buyer shall not rely on any quoted square footage and shall have the right to measure the Property.

C. TREATMENTS, REPAIRS AND REPLACEMENTS (TRR).

1) TERMITE TREATMENTS AND OTHER WOOD DESTROYING INSECTS. Seller's obligation to pay treatment and repair cost in relation to termites and other wood destroying insects shall be limited to the residential structure, garage(s) and other structures as designated in Paragraph 13 of the Contract and as provided in subparagraph C2b below.

2) TREATMENTS, REPAIRS, REPLACEMENTS AND REVIEWS. Buyer or Buyer's Broker, if applicable, within 24 hours after expiration of the time period referenced in Paragraph 7A of the Contract, shall deliver to Seller, in care of the Seller's Broker, if applicable, a copy of all written reports obtained by Buyer, if any, pertaining to the Property and Buyer shall select one of the following:

a. If, in the sole opinion of the Buyer, results of Investigations, Inspections or reviews are unsatisfactory, the Buyer may cancel the Contract by delivering written notice of cancellation to Seller, in care of Seller's Broker, if applicable, and receive refund of Earnest Money.

OR

b. Buyer, upon completion of all Investigations, Inspections and reviews, waives Buyer's right to cancel as provided in 7C2a above, by delivering to Seller, in care of Seller's Broker, if applicable, a written list on a

Notice of Treatments, repairs, and replacements form (TRR form) of those items to be treated, repaired or replaced (including repairs caused by termites and other wood destroying insects) that are not in normal working order (defined as the system or component functions without defect for the primary purpose and manner for which it was installed. Defect means a condition, malfunction or problem, which is not decorative, that will have a materially adverse effect on the value of a system or component).

c. Seller shall have _____ days (5 days if blank) after receipt of the completed TRR form from Seller's Broker, if applicable, to obtain costs estimates. Seller agrees to pay up to $_____ ("repair Cap") of costs of TRR's. If Seller, or Seller's Broker, if applicable, obtains cost estimates, which exceed repair Cap, Seller, or Seller's Broker, if applicable, shall notify Buyer or Buyer's Broker, if applicable, in writing, within two days after receipt of cost estimates. If the amount of the TRR's exceeds the amount of the repair Cap, Buyer and Seller shall have _____ days (3 days if blank) thereafter to negotiate the payment of costs in excess of repair Cap. If a written agreement is reached, Seller shall complete all agreed TRR's prior to the Closing Date. If an agreement is not reached within the time specified in this provision, the Contract shall become null and void and Earnest Money returned to Buyer.

d. If Seller fails to obtain cost estimates within the stated time, Buyer shall then have _____ days (5 days if blank) to:

e. Enter upon the Property to obtain costs estimates and require Seller to be responsible for all TRR's as noted on Buyer's TRR form, up to the repair Cap; and,

f. If the amount of the TRR's exceeds the amount of the repair Cap, Buyer and Seller shall have _____ days (3 days if blank) thereafter to negotiate the payment of costs in excess of repair Cap. If a written agreement is reached, Seller shall complete all agreed TRR's prior to the Closing Date. If an agreement is not reached within the time specified in this provision, the Contract shall become null and void and Earnest Money returned to Buyer.

D. EXPIRATION OF BUYER'S RIGHT TO CANCEL CONTRACT.

1) Failure of Buyer to complete one of the following shall constitute acceptance of the Property regardless of its condition: a. Perform any Investigations, Inspections or reviews; b. Deliver a written list on a TRR form of items to be treated, repaired and replaced; or c. Cancel the Contract within the time periods in Investigations, Inspections or reviews Paragraph.

2) After expiration of the time periods in Investigations, Inspections and reviews Paragraph, Buyer's inability to obtain a loan based on unavailability of hazard insurance coverage shall not relieve the Buyer of the obligation to close transaction.

3) After expiration of the time periods in Investigations, Inspections and reviews Paragraph, any square footage calculation of the dwelling, including but not limited to appraisal or survey, indicating more or less than quoted, shall not relieve the Buyer of the obligation to close this transaction.

E. INSPECTION OF TREATMENTS, REPAIRS AND REPLACEMENTS AND FINAL WALK-THROUGH.

1) Buyer, or other persons Buyer deems qualified, may perform re-inspections of Property pertaining to Treatments, repairs and replacements.
2) Buyer may perform a final walk-through inspection, which Seller may attend. Seller shall deliver Property in the same condition as it was on the date upon which Contract was signed by Buyer (ordinary wear and tear excepted) subject to Treatments, repairs and replacements.
3) All inspections and re-inspections shall be paid by Buyer, unless prohibited by mortgage lender.

8. RISK OF LOSS. Until transfer of Title or transfer of possession, risk of loss to the Property, ordinary wear and tear excepted, shall be upon Seller; after transfer of Title or transfer of possession, risk of loss shall be upon Buyer. (Parties are advised to address insurance coverage regarding transfer of possession prior to Closing.)

9. ACCEPTANCE OF PROPERTY. Buyer, upon accepting Title or transfer of possession of the Property, shall be deemed to have accepted the Property in its then condition. No warranties, expressed or implied, by Sellers, Brokers and/or their associated licensees, with reference to the condition of the Property, shall be deemed to survive the Closing.

10. TITLE EVIDENCE.

A. BUYER'S EXPENSE. Buyer, at Buyer's expense, shall obtain:

(Check one)

__ Attorney's Title Opinion, which is not rendered for Title Insurance purposes.

OR

__ Commitment for Issuance of a Title Insurance Policy based on an Attorney's Title opinion which is rendered for Title Insurance purposes for the owner's and Lender's Title Insurance Policy.

B. SELLER'S EXPENSE. Seller, at Seller's expense, within thirty (30) days prior to Closing Date, agrees to make available to Buyer the following (collectively referred to as "the Title Evidence"):

1) A complete surface-rights-only Abstract of Title, last certified to a date subsequent to the Time reference Date, by a licensed and bonded abstract company;

OR

2) A copy of Seller's existing owner's title insurance policy issued by a title insurer licensed in the State together with a supplement surface-rights-only abstract last certified to a date subsequent to the Time reference Date, by a licensed and bonded abstract company;

WITH

3) A current Uniform Commercial Code Search Certificate;

AND

4) An inspection certificate (commonly referred to as a "Mortgage Inspection Certificate") prepared subsequent to the Time reference Date by a licensed surveyor, which shall include a representation of the boundaries of the Property (without pin-stakes) and the improvements thereon.

C. LAND OR BOUNDARY SURVEY. By initialing this space _____, Buyer agrees to waive Seller's obligation to provide a Mortgage Inspection Certificate. Seller agrees that Buyer, at Buyer's expense, may have a licensed surveyor enter upon the Property to perform a Land or Boundary (Pin Stake) Survey, in lieu of a Mortgage Inspection Certificate, that shall then be considered as part of the Title Evidence.

D. BUYER TO EXAMINE TITLE EVIDENCE.

1) Buyer shall have ten (10) days after receipt to examine the Title Evidence and to deliver Buyer's objections to Title to Seller or Seller's Broker, if applicable. In the event the Title Evidence is not made available to Buyer within ten (10) days prior to Closing Date, said Closing Date shall be extended to allow Buyer the ten (10) days from receipt to examine the Title Evidence.

2) Buyer agrees to accept title subject to: (i) utility easements serving the property, (ii) building and use restrictions of record, (iii) set back and building lines, (iv) zoning regulations, and (v) reserved and severed mineral rights, which shall not be considered objections for requirements of Title.

E. SELLER TO CORRECT ISSUES WITH TITLE (IF APPLICABLE), POSSIBLE CLOSING DELAY. Upon receipt by Seller, or in care of Seller's Broker, if applicable, of any title requirements reflected in an Attorney's Title opinion or Title Insurance Commitment, based upon the standard of marketable title set out in accepted Title Examination Standards, the parties agree to the following:

1) Seller, at Seller's expense, shall make reasonable efforts to obtain and/or execute all documents necessary to cure title requirements identified by Buyer; and

2) Delay Closing Date for _____ days thirty (30) days if blank, or a longer period as may be agreed upon in writing, to allow Seller to cure Buyer's title requirements. In the event Seller cures Buyer's objection prior to the delayed Closing Date, Buyer and Seller agree to close within five (5) days of notice of such cure. In the event that title requirements are not cured within the time specified in this subparagraph, the Buyer may cancel the Contract and receive a refund of Earnest Money.

F. Upon Closing, any existing Abstract(s) of Title, owned by Seller, shall become the property of Buyer.

11. TAXES, ASSESSMENTS AND PRORATIONS.

A. General ad valorem taxes for the current calendar year shall be prorated through the date of closing, if certified. However, if the amount of such taxes has not been fixed, the proration shall be based upon the rate of levy for the previous calendar year and the most current assessed value available at the time of Closing.

B. The following items shall be paid by Seller at Closing: (i) Documentary Stamps; (ii) all utility bills, actual or estimated; (iii) all taxes other than general ad valorem taxes which are or may become a lien against the Property; (iv) any labor, materials, or other expenses related to the Property, incurred prior to Closing which is or may become a lien against the Property.

C. At Closing all leases, if any, shall be assigned to Buyer and security deposits, if any, shall be transferred to Buyer. Prepaid rent and lease payments shall be prorated through the date of Closing.

D. If applicable, membership and meters in utility districts to include, but not limited to, water, sewer, ambulance, fire, garbage, shall be transferred at no cost to Buyer at Closing.

E. If the property is subject to a mandatory Homeowner's Association, dues and assessments, if any, based on most recent assessment, shall be prorated through the date of Closing.

F. All governmental and municipal special assessments against the property (matured or not matured), not to include Homeowner's Association special assessments, whether or not payable in installments, shall be paid by Seller at Closing.

12. RESIDENTIAL SERVICE AGREEMENT. (CHECK ONE)

__ A. The Property shall not be covered by a residential Service Agreement

___ B. Seller currently has a residential Service Agreement in effect on the Property. Seller, at Seller's expense, shall transfer the agreement with one (1) year coverage to the Buyer at Closing.

___ C. The Property shall be covered by a residential Service Agreement selected by the Buyer at an approximate cost of $_____. Seller agrees to pay $_____ and Buyer agrees to pay the balance.

The Seller and Buyer acknowledge that the real estate broker(s) may receive a fee for services provided in connection with the residential Service Agreement. Buyer acknowledges that a residential Service Agreement does not replace/substitute Property inspection rights.

13. ADDITIONAL PROVISIONS.
_____.

14. MEDIATION. Any dispute arising with respect to the Contract shall first be submitted to a dispute resolution mediation system servicing the area in which the Property is located. Any settlement agreement shall be binding. In the event an agreement is not reached, the parties may pursue legal remedies as provided by the Contract.

15. BREACH AND FAILURE TO CLOSE

A. UPON BREACH BY SELLER. If the Buyer performs all of the obligations of Buyer, and if, within five (5) days after the date specified for Closing under Paragraph 3 of the Contract, Seller fails to convey the Title or fails to perform any other obligations of the Seller under this Contract, then Buyer shall be entitled to either cancel and terminate this Contract, return the abstract to Seller and receive a refund of the Earnest Money, or pursue any other remedy available at law or in equity, including specific performance.

B. UPON BREACH BY BUYER. If, after the Seller has performed Seller's obligation under this Contract, and if, within five (5) days after the date specified for Closing under Paragraph 3 of the Contract, the Buyer fails to provide funding, or to perform any other obligations of the Buyer under this Contract, then the Seller may, at Seller's option, cancel and terminate this Contract and retain all sums paid by the Buyer, but not to exceed 5% of the purchase price, as liquidated damages, or pursue any other remedy available at law or in equity, including specific performance.

16. INCURRED EXPENSES AND RELEASE OF EARNEST MONEY.

A. INCURRED EXPENSES. Buyer and Seller agree that any expenses, incurred on their behalf, shall be paid by the party incurring such expenses and shall not be paid from Earnest Money.

B. RELEASE OF EARNEST MONEY. In the event a dispute arises prior to the release of Earnest Money held in escrow, the escrow holder shall retain said Earnest Money until one of the following occur:

1) A written release is executed by Buyer and Seller agreeing to its disbursement;

2) Agreement of disbursement is reached through Mediation;

3) Interpleader or legal action is filed, at which time the Earnest Money shall be deposited with the Court Clerk; or

4) The passage of thirty (30) days from the date of final termination of the Contract has occurred and options 1), 2) or 3) above have not been exercised; Broker escrow holder, at Broker's discretion, may disburse Earnest Money. Such disbursement may be made only after fifteen (15) days written notice to Buyer and Seller at their last known address stating the escrow holder's proposed disbursement.

17. DELIVERY OF ACCEPTANCE OFOFFER OR COUNTER OFFER. The Buyer and Seller authorize their respective Brokers, if applicable, to receive delivery of an accepted offer or counteroffer.

18. NON-FOREIGN SELLER. Seller represents that at the time of acceptance of this contract and at the time of Closing, Seller is not a "foreign person" as such term is defined in the Foreign Investments in real Property Tax Act of 1980 (26 USC Section 1445(f) et. Sec) ("FIRPTA"). If either the sales price of the property exceeds $300,000.00 or the buyer does not intend to use the property as a primary residence then, at the Closing, and as a condition thereto, Seller shall furnish to Buyer an affidavit, in a form and substance acceptable to Buyer, signed under penalty of perjury containing Seller's United States Social Security and/or taxpayer identification numbers and a declaration to the effect that Seller is not a foreign person within the meaning of Section "FIRPTA."

19. EXECUTION BY PARTIES.

AGREED TO BY BUYER: on This Date_____

AGREED TO By SELLER: on This Date_____

Buyer's Printed Name   Seller's Printed Name

_____   _____

Buyer's Signature   Seller's Signature

_____   _____

TERMINATION OF OFFER

The above offer shall automatically terminate on _____ at
__:00 p.m., unless withdrawn prior to acceptance or termination.

EARNEST MONEY RECEIPT AND INSTRUCTIONS

The receipt of $_____ Check Cash as Earnest Money Deposit, to be deposited in accordance with the terms and conditions of PURCHASE PRICE, EARNEST MONEY, AND SOURCE OF FUNDS Paragraph. Broker(s) acknowledges receipt of Earnest Money and Listing Broker, if applicable, shall deposit said funds in accordance with Paragraph 2 of this Contract. If deposited in an escrow account other than the Listing Broker, the Listing Broker, if applicable, shall provide a copy of receipt to the Selling Broker.